CLOUD
COMPUTING

The MIT Press Essential Knowledge Series

CLOUD COMPUTING

NAYAN B. RUPARELIA

The MIT Press | Cambridge, Massachusetts | London, England

Set in Chaparral Pro by the MIT Press. Printed on acid-free and SFI-certified paper, and bound in the United States of America.

Library of Congress Cataloging-in-Publication Data

Names: Ruparelia, Nayan, author.
Title: Cloud computing / Nayan Ruparelia.
Description: Cambridge, MA : The MIT Press, [2015] | Series: The MIT Press essential knowledge series | Includes bibliographical references and index.
Identifiers: LCCN 2015039870 | ISBN 9780262529099 (pbk. : alk. paper)
Subjects: LCSH: Cloud computing. | Cloud computing--Security measures.
Classification: LCC QA76.585 .R87 2015 | DDC 004.67/82--dc23 LC record available at http://lccn.loc.gov/2015039870

10   9   8   7   6   5   4   3   2   1

CONTENTS

SERIES FOREWORD

The MIT Press Essential Knowledge series offers accessible, concise, beautifully produced pocket-size books on topics of current interest. Written by leading thinkers, the books in this series deliver expert overviews of subjects that range from the cultural and the historical to the scientific and the technical.

In today's era of instant information gratification, we have ready access to opinions, rationalizations, and superficial descriptions. Much harder to come by is the foundational knowledge that informs a principled understanding of the world. Essential Knowledge books fill that need. Synthesizing specialized subject matter for nonspecialists and engaging critical topics through fundamentals, each of these compact volumes offers readers a point of access to complex ideas.

Bruce Tidor
Professor of Biological Engineering and Computer Science
Massachusetts Institute of Technology

PREFACE

Not many people know what cloud computing is. Despite the hundreds of books and articles that have been written on the topic, few actually understand cloud computing. Sometimes, I feel, this applies to even the authors themselves. One of the reasons is that most of the books and articles discuss cloud computing from a highly technical viewpoint, instead of a user's one. Another is the marketing hype that various businesses have created to use cloud computing as a selling point. This has led to a lot of confusion. This situation is common whenever a new technology enters the fray, and especially one that is bound to create a major paradigm shift. The purpose of this book therefore is to cut through the hype and show you how you can take advantage of cloud computing.

You could be an investor who wants to learn more about the cloud-based technologies produced by the business you invest in, an entrepreneur who wants to use cloud computing to ramp up your start-up in an agile manner, a lawyer or judge working on a case that relates to cloud computing, a technologist who wants to use cloud computing in a new product or service that you are defining, a business student who wants to understand the paradigm shift that cloud computing represents to businesses globally, or a layperson who is curious about the subject—this book is for you. This book will help you understand cloud computing from a user's standpoint: when to use it and when not to, how to select a cloud service and how to incorporate it with other cloud services or traditional IT, and what best practice is when using cloud computing.

As far as possible, I have refrained from considering commercial cloud services or offerings in this book for three main reasons: (1) if one is not careful, the book can become an advertisement for various cloud service providers; (2) some vendors are here today and gone tomorrow, as is the nature within the fast-paced technology industry; and (3) the principal aim of this book is to provide concepts that will equip you to better make your own decisions about such offerings in the first place.

This is not a technical book. It is a book written primarily for a nonspecialist, although a technical specialist should benefit from reading this book in order to understand the broader impact and considerations of cloud computing. Thus no prior knowledge of cloud computing or any of its related technologies is required in reading this book. I advise strongly, however, that you read the first chapter of this book first so that we may have a shared, common vocabulary and understanding of cloud computing. This will prove useful when you read the succeeding chapters. You may read any of the chapters of the book in any order after going through the first chapter.

Roadmap

Chapter 1 provides an overview of cloud computing. It provides a definition and discusses each component that makes up that definition. It also considers the merits of cloud computing and provides a brief idea of some of its applications. It concludes with a discussion of the various players, or stakeholders, that participate in the cloud computing value chain.

Chapter 2 builds on the introduction of chapter 1 by describing the types of cloud computing in terms of its abstraction and deployment models. It further compares and contrasts the models' component characteristics using new concepts that I have developed such as cloud patterns and cloud cells. These show how specialist clouds can be built, or used, in order to address specific use cases. Concepts from object-oriented design (OOD) are then borrowed to create relationships between these specialist clouds, called cloud cells. Thus a large variety of clouds for various use cases can be built by re-using the cloud cells and defining their interrelationships. This culminates with the discussion of use case patterns.

Chapter 3 asks a pertinent question: why cloud computing? What benefits does it provide, when should you use it, and what impact will it have on you, your work, your society, and your life? The chapter considers various concepts such as the personal cloud and the cloud of things.

Chapter 4 is a more objective version of chapter 3, especially from a financial perspective. This chapter will help you understand the various price models that cloud vendors can have. It is your toolkit for comparing price and value received from different cloud services and their vendors.

Chapter 5 considers Security and Governance. Not only is this subject topical given the various security breaches we have heard about, but is especially important when considering cloud computing. Topics such as security containers, monitoring, data integrity, data loss prevention, data privacy, data sovereignty, and legal and compliance issues are considered. Appended to the chapter is a section that explains common security terms used by specialists within the industry.

Chapters 6 to 9 inclusive consider use case patterns that were first introduced as a concept in chapter 2. The patterns are discussed in terms of the various abstraction levels of cloud computing: (a) Infrastructure and Platform, (b) Software, (c) Information, and (d) Business Process. These four chapters share a common template: examples of use case patterns are discussed for the abstraction level followed by a SWOT analysis and a key take-away section.

Chapter 10 considers transitioning to the cloud. Once you have decided upon the cloud offering, what is the best practice for you to transition a legacy service to a cloud service? The chapter answers this key question by considering cloud usage models, interoperability, critical success factors and a cloud maturity model.

Chapter 11, entitled Future Outlook, discusses emerging technologies associated with as well as peripheral to cloud computing that will have an impact upon the future of cloud computing. New concepts such as a cloud service exchange (not the same as cloud exchanges) and cloud of things are introduced in the chapter.

Chapter 12 provides my personal opinion on various aspects of our society that I feel will be impacted by cloud computing specifically and emergent technologies generally. Using trends and practices outlined in Huxley's *Brave New World Revisited* and Bernays's *Propaganda* as background, I present my thoughts on the social, business and personal landscape that technology affects.

A glossary is provided at the end of the book for some of the main terms and acronyms used in cloud computing.

ACKNOWLEDGMENTS

It took a long time for me to write this book. A whole year went by because my responsibilities increased at work and my workload was such that I had few evenings or weekends free to work on the manuscript. I was finally able to complete around 90 percent of the manuscript when disaster struck: I lost my entire manuscript because of a silly oversight on my part when upgrading my computer's system disk. This despite my having a network attached storage (NAS) server that I had built with umpteen amounts of hardware redundancy. The Achilles' heel, as so often happens, was the software I had used for backup and restore. Anyway, most of the manuscript had to be re-written. Because practice makes perfect, I believe that this second manuscript is much better than the first. My backup-restore incident was in fact what prompted me to write about backup and restore processes (see the appendix), so that the same situation may not happen to you. Throughout all this, the publishers, and especially Marc Lowenthal and Marie Lee, stood firmly by me. Without their faith and patience, this book would never have seen the light of day. I should also like to thank Kathleen Hensley, Deborah Cantor-Adams, and Nancy Wolfe Kotary for their assistance in improving the quality of this book.

INTRODUCTION

Consider a typical work day that you spend using your computer. How much of your computer's resources do you actually use at peak usage times? The average for most users is about 10 percent of the processor, 60 percent of memory, and 20 percent of network bandwidth. (That is at peak usage; the normal usage levels during work hours are considerably less, on average.) Nevertheless, you paid for 100 percent of the resources, up front, when you bought your computer. Your networking costs are not different in nature either because most Internet service providers (ISPs) have a lock-in period that commits you to their customer base for at least a year. Suppose that your workplace has hundreds or even thousands of computers that are used at a nominal rate: would it not be good to pool the unused computing resources of all the company's computers and put them to good use? That way, your company gets the biggest bang for its buck. Let us now transpose the same thinking to the data center where there are numerous servers—such as web servers, application servers, and database servers—being used in a similar manner at minimal usage rates. These too could have their hardware resources pooled and shared across servers so that you could utilize them more efficiently; otherwise, as in figure 1, you will need to invest up front for computing resources that may only be used occasionally. The extra pooled resources that

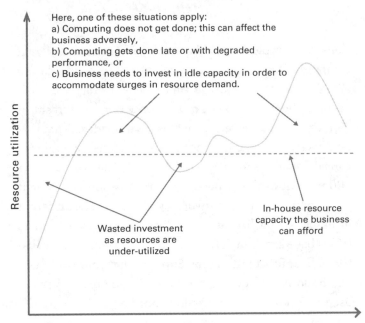

Figure 1　Investment problem solved by cloud computing

are unused by you could then be used by others in your company via your company's network. Alternatively, if your company appoints a third party to provide resource pooling, then you would access your computing resources over the Internet.

But, what if your company or department only paid for the computing resources that it uses? Then your company would not have to invest up front, as capital expenditure, in purchasing the computing but simply sign up with a service provider on a pay-as-you-use billing model. This effectively means that your company changes from a capital expenditure (CapEx) model to an operating expenditure (OpEx) one for meeting its computing needs. This is where cloud computing comes in.

A Definition of Cloud Computing

Although information technology (IT) has become ubiquitous at home and at work today, the industry is still in its infancy. And cloud computing, one of the latest IT innovations, is still in its formative stage. Inevitably, during the formative stage of a technology, a lot of attention is given to it to the extent that it borders on hype. Consequently, everyone, from the technologist to the salesperson, is keen to jump onto the bandwagon by labeling anything with the remotest resemblance (often exaggerated or extrapolated) to cloud computing as being part of the cloud computing domain. This creates obfuscation. Thus, a number of definitions abound for cloud computing. The best definition is from the National Institute of Standards and Technology (NIST), a technology agency that is part of the US Department of Commerce that works with industry to develop and apply technology, measurements, and standards. The NIST definition of cloud computing[1] is:

> Cloud computing is a model for enabling ubiquitous, convenient, on-demand network access to a shared pool of configurable computing resources (e.g., networks, servers, storage, applications, and services) that can be rapidly provisioned and released with minimal management effort or service provider interaction. This cloud model promotes availability and is composed of five essential characteristics, three service models, and four deployment models.

Although the NIST definition needs updating, especially with regard to the three service models that we will examine shortly in this chapter, it is the best definition at present. In essence we will use NIST's definition to describe, one by one, the essential characteristics, deployment models, and service models of cloud computing.

Before delving into the characteristics of cloud computing, let us first delve into virtualization and cloud services because these form the basis of cloud computing in two distinct manners. First, from a technical perspective: virtualization; second, from a conceptual perspective: cloud services.

Virtualization

Cloud computing relies on virtualization technology. There are two basic types of virtualization: server virtualization and application virtualization. Application virtualization delivers an application that is hosted on a single machine to a large number of users. The application can be situated in the cloud on high-grade virtual machines but, because a large number of users access it, its costs are shared by those users. This makes the application cheaper to deliver to the end user. The end user does not need to have high-grade hardware in order to run the application; an inexpensive machine, such as a low-end workstation or a thin-client terminal, will suffice. And if the data used by the virtual application are stored in the cloud, the user is not tethered to any one device or location to use the application or access its data. Typically, in such cases, the virtual application is consumed through a mobile app or an Internet browser by the end user.

Server virtualization uses common physical hardware (networks, storage or computing machines) to host virtual machines. A physical host machine could have any number of virtual machines running on it so that one set of hardware is used to run different machines. Virtual machines can be installed with their own operating system and their own different set of applications; the operating systems or applications do not need to be the same across the virtual machines. Server virtualization has a major cost benefit: it allows you to consolidate a large number of physical machines onto fewer physical machines that host the virtual machines. This increase in computing efficiency results in lower space, maintenance, cooling, and electricity costs, besides the obvious reduction in procurement costs for the machines. An additional benefit is that fewer physical machines and lower electricity bills translate to environment friendliness.

When you pool the virtual machines together such that they may be instantiated (activated and switched on) instantaneously in a manner where they may join or leave the pool, you have a situation where you can scale your resources to meet any change—either an increase or decrease—in demand. This instantaneous change in the number of virtual machines within a pool is known as elasticity, which is made possible in a cost efficient manner due to server virtualization.

Now, what is different between virtualization and cloud computing? Let us recall from the NIST definition for cloud computing these characteristics: on-demand self-service, rapid elasticity, and measured service provision.

None of these are provided as a matter of course by virtualization. Virtualization can act as an enabling technology in order to facilitate these features, but a lot of additional enablers are required such as reporting, billing, demand management, and various other business processes and tools. To truly deploy a cloud, you need to consider how to standardize your service offerings, make them available through simple portals, track usage and cost information, measure their availability, orchestrate them to meet demand, provide a security framework, provide instantaneous reporting, and have a billing or charging mechanism on the basis of usage. Another way of looking at this is that virtualization, per se, is not a service. It can be used, in conjunction with other tools and processes, to create an infrastructure-as-a-service offering.

Cloud Services

Let us examine what constitutes a service—specifically a cloud service—by employing the analogy of an accountancy firm. Suppose that you want your accounts managed and you appoint an accountancy firm. Let us postulate your main criteria for selecting the firm:

1.   integrity and reputation of the firm (you want your accounts to be accurate, and you do not want your accounts released to the world!),

To truly deploy a cloud, you need to consider how to standardize your service offerings, make them available through simple portals, track usage and cost information, measure their availability, orchestrate them to meet demand, provide a security framework, provide instantaneous reporting, and have a billing or charging mechanism on the basis of usage.

2. promptness in preparing the accounts and lowering your tax bill (the benefits that you will receive), and

3. fees the firm will charge (the cost of realizing the benefits).

You are not likely to care about the number of employees the firm will employ in preparing your accounts, the software used, or the computers the software will be installed on. Rather, your interest will be in the firm's service and its benefits. These service benefits form a contract, a bond between you and the accountancy firm in a written or unwritten format; such a contract is called a service level agreement (SLA).

In IT, a service is a collection of IT systems, components, and resources that work together to provide value to users. An important element of this is that, in order to measure and agree upon the value received, two parameters are usually used to assess a service: cost and the SLA. The SLA is essentially a contract between the service consumer and the service supplier in terms of how quickly the service will be delivered (when), its quality (what), and scope (where and how much). Notice that these parameters represent the benefit that accrues to the service consumer. If the service consumer happens to be internal to the company, say a marketing department, then the internal agreement between the supplier and consumer departments of that company is called an operational level agreement (OLA). A cloud service therefore is *the implementation of a business process—provided through a set of related functional components and resources—that provides business value to its consumers.*

Continuing this analogy, suppose that the accountancy firm wishes to ensure that it meets the SLA agreed with you. It could put in place various metrics internally that it could measure to monitor its performance while creating the accounts. For example, the metrics could be that the audit needs to take three days or the cash book needs to be reconciled within a week. The firm may agree to share these metrics with you, although usually they are used internally as objectives to ensure that they will meet the overall SLA. These objectives, or metrics, are referred to as service level objectives (SLOs). From an IT standpoint, SLOs are specific measurable characteristics of the SLA such as uptime, throughput, available resource capacity, response time, and delivery time.

Service Models: Levels of Abstraction

Now let us look at IT from the accountancy firm's perspective. The IT department at the firm has that firm's accountants as its customers. These accountants have a choice in the way they interact with their IT department:

1.   They could get down to the nitty gritty and specify the hardware and software in terms of the type and version of software to use, the operating system that hosts the software, the hardware's memory, storage space, and so on and on.

2.   They could specify the software they wish to use and let the IT department figure out the rest.

3.   They could simply agree the type of input data they would like to have computed and the format of the resulting dataset, and leave it to the IT department to use whatever software and hardware it wanted to employ in order to compute the data.

Item 1 is a level of abstraction at the infrastructure layer. In cloud computing, it is known as infrastructure as a service (IaaS). Common examples of IaaS are when you store data, files, or pictures in the cloud (this uses the storage infrastructure) or use the cloud to transfer files. A higher level of abstraction is when the IT department provides a platform, complete with hardware and operating system, and the accountants specify the software to use, as in item 2 above. This is platform as a service (PaaS).

If the IT department were required to decide the right software and computing platform to use on behalf of the accountants, as in item 3, such that the accountants only need to care about the accuracy and timeliness of the data returned to them, that level of abstraction would be software as a service (SaaS). These three abstraction levels (IaaS, PaaS, and SaaS) are the service models referred to in the NIST definition.

What if our accountancy firm decided to outsource the entire auditing function to another firm so that they could concentrate on advising you on tax matters? Our firm would agree to an SLA and the cost with the other firm, which would then audit the accounts accordingly. This amounts to outsourcing an entire business function, or process, to another firm. That other firm could just as well be replaced by a cloud service. Thus the cloud service, when providing a business function, is providing a business process as a service (BPaaS).

Suppose that in order to obtain the latest tax regulations, an information service could be provided to our accountancy firm. This would be akin to information as a service (INaaS). Since the tax codes and regulations are updated regularly as the law changes, this is a service that relies on not only the storage of data, which would then be IaaS, but also on the manipulation of that data to provide meaningful information. Hence INaaS is distinct from IaaS.

The NIST model therefore needs to be updated with these two service abstractions: INaaS and BPaaS, as figure 2 illustrates.

IT enterprise architecture recognizes four architecture domains, as shown in the left column of figure 2. These are technology architecture, applications architecture,

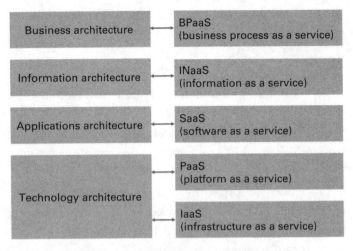

Figure 2 Enterprise architecture stack and cloud service models

information or data architecture, and business architecture. Technology architecture encompasses IT infrastructure, middleware, and operating systems; applications architecture concerns software applications, their interactions and relationships with business processes; data architecture defines the data assets and their management; business architecture translates the business strategy to an IT strategy, relevant governance framework and definition of business processes. Each of these domains in the enterprise architecture stack maps to and aligns with the cloud service models that are shown in the right column of figure 2.

Cloud Deployment Models

The NIST definition contains four distinct deployment models: public, private, community, and hybrid clouds.

A public cloud provides services to anyone having Internet access. Such a service may be provided by computing resources located anywhere in the world. This type of cloud has the disadvantage of data integrity for some companies for regulatory reasons. For example, companies based in the United States are not allowed to store consumer data in other countries. Financial institutions, especially, need to comply with strict regulations of this nature. As a result such companies usually tend to favor private clouds.

A private cloud is one that provides services to a single entity, either a government organization or a business enterprise, such that cloud services are provided to that entity from its own private network. Usually only large enterprises can afford to have private clouds. Small or medium enterprises have the option of a community cloud.

A community cloud is one that provides a middle ground between a private cloud and a public one. A number of entities, ranging from individuals to enterprises, which have a common interest can pool their resources to create a hybrid cloud. Such clouds take various shapes: a banking cloud in Switzerland serving the cantonal banks (Switzerland is divided into administrative units called cantons), a paper industry cloud in the Nordics, or a health cloud for the health industry in the United States. However, one could also have community clouds for various interest groups, for instance, for chess players and numismatists.

A hybrid cloud is essentially a conglomeration of the other types of clouds. Its use is mostly necessary when a cloud service needs to peruse computing resources from other clouds because its own resources are being utilized at full capacity. Such a concept is known as cloud bursting because the service bursts out of its cloud to utilize resources from other clouds in order to meet its service level agreement.

Five Characteristics of Cloud Computing

The NIST definition lists five characteristics of cloud computing, as listed in the second column of table 1: ubiquitous access, on-demand availability based on the consumer's self-service, pooling of resources, rapid elasticity, and measured service usage.

Ubiquitous access through a network is important because you are not constrained by where you are in order to use the cloud service; a concomitant concern is that, as the potential user base increases, so does the danger of security being compromised. For this reason network access may be limited to a private network or a community of users. The former translates to a private cloud and the latter to a community cloud model.

Table 1 Characteristics of cloud computing

	Characteristic	Description	Parameter
1	Broad network access	Consume services from anywhere	Where
2	On-demand self-service	Consume services when you want	When
3	Resource pooling and virtualization	Pool the infrastructure, virtual platforms, and applications	How
4	Rapid elasticity	Share pooled resources to enable horizontal scalability	How
5	Measured service	Pay for the service you consume as you consume it	How much

On-demand self-service, or on-demand availability, has the advantage of empowering you to consume the service whenever you want. Availability has two characteristics here:

1. the service will be available to you even when you are not using it so that it will be ready for you to use when you request it (thus the up-time of the cloud computing services has to be very good), and

2. the service remains available while you are using it (thus your user experience should not be impaired even if there may be an upsurge in the number of users).

The latter aspect means that, regardless of the varying demands you place on the service, it should remain available to you. For example, you could have an IaaS cloud service on which you host your website and its usage levels will vary according to the hits the site receives. The usage, in turn, will depend on a number of factors such as the time of day, whether it is a weekend, or if you have a marketing campaign running. As a result the load placed upon the cloud computing infrastructure will also vary, and the infrastructure will need to scale out when greater demand is placed on it; likewise, it would scale in when there is less demand so that the infrastructure resources can be used elsewhere. This scaling in and out is known as *elasticity*.

Horizontal scalability is when you use greater numbers of the same type of resources, say computing platforms, in order to meet demand. Vertical scalability is when you improve the performance of those resources by upgrading them, for example, increasing the amount of memory. Elasticity is when you use horizontal scalability to scale out when demand is high and then scale in when it is low. In order to implement this, computing resources are pooled. The resources normally tend to be virtualized because you can use software to pool and scale them automatically. Usually, virtualization allows you to run multiple, independent instances of operating systems on a single physical computer, as figure 3 illustrates; such virtual systems are referred to as virtual machines. However, at the infrastructure level, you can have virtual storage (multiple storage volumes on a single physical storage device) and virtual networks in addition to virtual machines.

Virtualizing the hardware allows you to pool and share the resources in an elastic manner. And the same thinking can be extrapolated to software so that you could have virtual applications that can be shared even though a single instance of the software runs on the pooled virtual machines. This technology, however, is still in its formative stage as the biggest constraints are commercial issues such as the licensing arrangements and billing model. When multiple users use the same virtual resources in the cloud, such as the software, storage, or virtual machines, those resources have multiple tenants. The pooling of resources to provide a shared, common, service to each user of the cloud service is known as multi-tenancy.

A major disadvantage of current public cloud services is a lack of transparency[2] in terms of the resources consumed

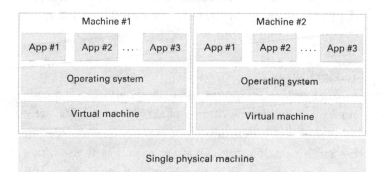

Figure 3 Physical machine hosting virtual machines

and the costs incurred. Yet these are distinct characteristics of cloud computing insofar as the consumer ought to know what computing resources are being consumed, as and when they are consumed, and the instantaneous concomitant costs of the consumption. (Of course, this factor becomes less relevant if the charging model is based on a "consume as much as you want" pay monthly basis.) That is why it is important for a cloud service to measure the consumption of that service and to make that metric transparent to the user.

Cloud Computing Actors

The creation, delivery, and consumption of cloud services have four distinct participants, or actors, that interact in the supply chain, as illustrated in figure 4. These four entities are described in this section.

Service Consumer

A cloud service consumer uses cloud services. The consumer usually keeps a catalog of services that he is likely to consume. In order for a cloud service to be included in the service catalog, the consumer examines the service's characteristics such as cost, quality, and timeliness—and reaches an agreement on these with the cloud service provider.

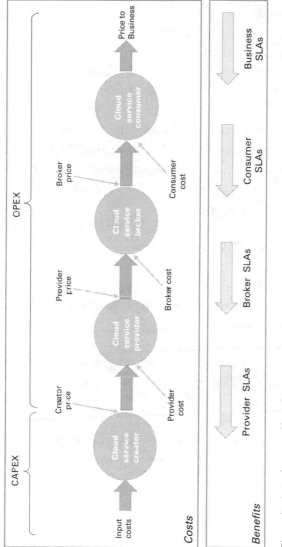

Figure 4 Actors' costs and benefits

Service Provider

A cloud service provider is an entity that provides cloud services to the cloud service consumer. In doing so he orchestrates the configuration and activation of services to the consumer in a timely—almost instantaneous—manner. The service provider may also maintain a service catalog of the services being provided, together with the cost and contractual information. In this regard, the provider makes a distinction with regard to a service's cost and price. The former is the input cost, or the dollar amount he, as the service provider, needs to bear in order to provide the service profitably; the latter is the dollar amount charged to the service consumer.

Service Creator

A service provider may optionally act as a service creator. A service creator creates the service and supplies it to the service provider. The main function of the service creator, when supplying a service to the provider, is to marshal and optimize the supply of resources that underpin a service.

Service Broker

A service broker acts as an intermediary between a service consumer and a number of service providers. The broker plays three distinct roles:

1.   prevents a consumer from being locked in to a particular provider so that the consumer may use different providers for the same service,

2.   aggregates services from various providers and provides a unique service to the consumer that is a "mash-up," or composition, of various services, and

3.   orchestrates the services to the consumer from a number of providers based on the optimum cost, quality, and timeliness parameters.

The broker makes the same cost and price distinction for the services as the provider. Thus, in essence, the provider's price becomes the broker's cost and the broker's price becomes the consumer's cost. Similarly, the SLAs represent the benefits and these accrue across the chain, as in figure 4, from the cloud service creator through to the consumer.

TYPES OF CLOUD COMPUTING

The previous chapter touched upon two key characteristics of cloud services: service abstraction levels (IaaS, PaaS, SaaS, InaaS, and BPaaS) and deployment models (public, private, hybrid, and community clouds). This chapter delves deeper into the abstraction and deployment models. We will compare and contrast their component characteristics and build a number of paradigms in cloud computing based on cloud relationships.

Remember the definition of cloud computing from the previous chapter? Cloud computing has five key properties:

1.   broad network access,

2.   on-demand self-service,

3.   resource pooling or shared services,

4. rapid elasticity, and

5. measured service.

Every single one of these properties needs to be present for a service to qualify as a cloud service. It is very important to understand this because, otherwise, it is just not a cloud service despite the claims made by would-be cloud service providers. Also, the discussion in this chapter will then not necessarily apply. As such, all the deployment models and abstraction levels that we consider in this chapter have in common these five properties of cloud computing.

First, there are a few new concepts that I have developed that we need to consider in the analysis of cloud computing. One such concept is borrowed from object-oriented design (OOD) principles in terms of object relationships. Another concept is that of a cloud cell. This is a specialist cloud that does only one thing, such as data storage, providing a database service, or serving web pages, for example. You can create a cloud application that uses a number of cloud cells to create a cloud service that you can use. This novel concept means that you can re-use a number of cells and, through various combinations and relationships, create a variety of cloud services. We can extend this approach further by creating cloud patterns. These are distinct use cases based on a combination of cloud cells and their relationships.

Abstraction Levels

Service models can be viewed in terms of increased levels of abstraction. As you move up the stack to the top, you have the highest form of abstraction at the business process-as-a-service (BPaaS) level. This is illustrated in figure 5.

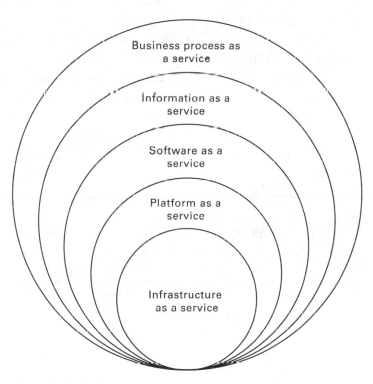

Figure 5 Levels of abstraction

Notice that each higher level incorporates the levels below it. That is to say, software as a service (SaaS) incorporates software that provides a business function and at the same time provides a platform as a service (PaaS). And platform as a service provides an operating environment in addition to infrastructure as a service (IaaS). Table 2 lists the definitions of the five abstraction levels of cloud computing in terms of the service offerings.

Notice in the table the distinctions between the abstraction levels. It is easy to mistake one service for another, especially when marketing departments of different cloud service providers come to be adventurous in stretching the definitions. For example, suppose you are provided with IaaS. The service provider will pre-install the operating system for you because they do not wish you to have access to the infrastructure for security reasons, the service offered is still IaaS, not PaaS, even though it has an operating system installed. For it to be PaaS, the service provider would additionally need to install requisite software that your application will require in order for it to run. This additional software can be software libraries that perform set tasks, a framework such as .Net that includes a standard set of libraries, or even an application stack such as LAMP (Linux-Apache-MySQL-PHP or Perl) that includes a web server (Apache), a database (MySQL), and a programming language with its libraries (PHP or Perl) hosted on a Linux server. Once you use the IaaS (or the PaaS) service to write

Table 2 Service offerings for different abstraction levels

Abstraction level	Service offering
Infrastructure as a service (IaaS)	Hardware infrastructure (servers, storage, etc.) on a utility basis.
Platform as a service (PaaS)	Same as IaaS but includes the operating system and any other core applications of the operating environment to enable you to install and run your software. Pricing generally is on a utility basis.
Software as a service (SaaS)	As per PaaS but includes hosted applications that fulfill a function. The function could be a business, social, or personal function. You simply use the application or applications that you need, when you need it, and avoid the cost of installing and maintaining the application and its supporting hardware infrastructure. Pricing is on a per-use basis.
Information as a service (INaaS)	Provides information relevant to an individual or corporation and to their businesses, business processes, or tasks. Pricing is usually on a consumption, per-use basis.
Business process as a service (BPaaS)	Fulfills a business function or replaces a business process in an organization. Typically combines business process outsourcing (BPO) with software as a service (SaaS). Pricing generally on a per use basis.

your application, you can host it in the cloud and offer it as SaaS—software as a service. That way, your customers do not have to worry about installing the application, the operating system it runs on, or any of your application's software dependencies. More crucially, they do not have to worry about keeping the software current because you will install the latest version with your SaaS offering.

Deployment Models

Recall from chapter 1 the four deployment models of cloud computing: public, private, community, and hybrid. Each deployment model additionally has an abstraction level that describes it. For example, a public cloud having an abstraction level of SaaS would be described as *SaaS Public Cloud*. Likewise a *PaaS Private Cloud* would be a cloud that has a private deployment model and a PaaS abstraction level, and so on.

Public Clouds

A public cloud, as its name suggests, is available to the public at large. In this regard, the public can be a consumer or an organization that wants to use cloud services. The consumption of public cloud services is almost always via the Internet rather than a private or restricted network. The public cloud is the deployment model that most people are familiar with. The public cloud has applicability across the various abstraction levels. As such, you will find public clouds that provide infrastructure, platform, software, information, or business processes as a service. Whereas cloud services of the other deployment models may be accessed via networks that can be local, wide, or worldwide (the Internet), the public cloud model is almost always only available via the Internet with a monthly charge for use. Examples of a public cloud service include Google Print, Google Docs, Microsoft Office 365, Amazon EC2, and Amazon Cloud Player among others. These all have a monthly operating expenditure price model in common and have little or no up-front capital expenditure costs borne by the consumer.

Private Clouds

A private cloud has as its scope an organization, business unit, or even a single person. A company can have its own private cloud that delivers services over its wide area network (WAN). You can think of a WAN as a companywide Internet that restricts outsiders through the use of security devices such as firewalls. A local area network (LAN) is similar to a WAN except that it is much smaller in its geographic scope: it normally is restricted to a particular site such as a home or a business location. A person could have his own private cloud in order to consume services over a LAN. For example, a home can have its own cloud that (1) connects a streaming server to a video set-top box so that videos can be watched, recorded, or played back from anywhere in the house; (2) provides a backup server to store files centrally; and (3) a synchronization service that synchronizes data across devices (laptops, mobile phones, tablets, etc.) using a wireless LAN.

A private cloud is therefore one that delivers services over a LAN or a WAN and restricts consumption of those services to a select group of users. In limited circumstances, private cloud services may be delivered via the Internet, but with access restrictions so that only private entities can gain access to those services. In practice, data integrity and security issues can make service delivery over the Internet difficult for private clouds. Generally, private clouds have a non-recurring component, and they also have an operating expenditure component.

Community Clouds

The community cloud is a broader version of a private cloud. It supports a community that has common interests or shared concerns such as security requirements, data privacy, regulatory environment, business model, and needs of end users. A community cloud can even have a geographical region as its scope, for example, a European Union community cloud or a North American cloud. It can have trade as its scope, for example, an ASEAN or a BRIC community cloud. The trade concept is quite interesting because it can be extended to any number of industries or business groups: a paper industry cloud, a publishing cloud, a banking regulation cloud, a health industry cloud that may be specific to a country (e.g., a US Health Community Cloud) or to the industry vertical globally (e.g., a Worldwide Health Community Cloud), and then have as its participants regulatory bodies, health providers, practitioners, and consumers, or any combination of these.

The community cloud shares the same cloud infrastructure if it is an IaaS community cloud, the same cloud software if it is a SaaS community, or the same cloud business processes if it is a BPaaS community cloud. Unlike a private cloud, community cloud services are usually delivered over the Internet and generally have an operating expenditure price model.

Hybrid Clouds

A hybrid cloud is an encapsulation (see the section on encapsulation below) of two or more cloud deployment models (private, community, or public) that has its own unique characteristics. The hybrid cloud can be made up of a single deployment model, as in *Hybrid Cloud 1* of figure 6, which is a hybrid cloud comprised of three private clouds; it can equally well be composed of public clouds instead. The deployment model does not need to be the same. You can have a hybrid cloud consisting of different models, as is the case for *Hybrid Cloud 2*, which has a private and a public cloud. Then again, hybrid clouds can have community clouds as in the case *Hybrid Cloud 3* of figure 6. There can even be a hybrid cloud within a hybrid cloud, as in *Hybrid Cloud 4*, so that you could have a replica of the other component clouds within your inner hybrid cloud for purposes of business continuity or load balancing.

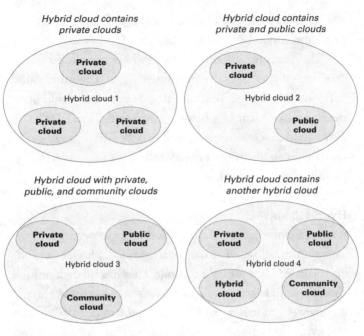

*Hybrid cloud contains
private clouds*

*Hybrid cloud contains
private and public clouds*

**Private
cloud**

Hybrid cloud 1

**Private
cloud**

**Private
cloud**

**Private
cloud**

Hybrid cloud 2

**Public
cloud**

*Hybrid cloud with private,
public, and community clouds*

*Hybrid cloud contains
another hybrid cloud*

**Private
cloud**

**Public
cloud**

Hybrid cloud 3

**Community
cloud**

**Private
cloud**

**Public
cloud**

Hybrid cloud 4

**Hybrid
cloud**

**Community
cloud**

Figure 6 Varieties of hybrid clouds

Can the component clouds of a hybrid cloud be of any abstraction level? For instance, can you have a private cloud that is IaaS and a public cloud that is PaaS within a hybrid cloud? Absolutely! Let us consider an example of such a case by re-visiting our accountancy firm. Suppose that our firm wants to make use of public cloud services for customer relationship management (CRM), mail, and word processing using commonly available commercial public cloud services but at the same time has some business applications such as inventory-tracking software that are available in its own private cloud. Our firm could create a hybrid cloud such that some of the data can be shared between the public and private clouds, for example, supplier addresses. This would allow the public cloud's word processing to send letters to suppliers and at the same time allow the private cloud's inventory tracker to assess which supplier ought to be contacted in order to replenish stock. What are the advantages of such a hybrid cloud? The private cloud provides data privacy, greater performance, and transparent service level objectives; the public cloud provides standard services that grant it flexibility and cost efficiency, as our firm does not have to re-invent the wheel by having to create its own word-processing cloud services.

Types of Cloud

Clouds can take the form of any deployment model. You can deploy your type of personal cloud as a private cloud. Dropbox is an example of a public cloud deployment model that can be used as a personal cloud for files. In this section we will consider the personal cloud and the cloud of things as two distinct types of cloud.

Personal Cloud

A personal cloud is defined by its scope rather than whether or not it is available on a shared basis. Recall that this cloud's scope is a person or a single entity, and that it can be a private, public, or hybrid cloud. Examples of *public* personal clouds are iCloud, Google Drive, and Dropbox. An example of a *private* personal cloud is a network attached storage device that backs up your data; Apple's Airport Time Capsule, when connected to more than one device, is an implementation of this.

Cloud of Things

A cloud of things has inanimate objects, or things, as its scope; that is, it is a cloud that works with things instead of people or organizations. For example, you can have a cloud of public lighting—such as street or car park lighting—operated on a pay-per-use basis so that the lighting is available only to those who have paid for it and are in the vicinity. The lights therefore turn on when someone is in the vicinity and turn off when they leave; the amount charged would depend on the length of time they are in the vicinity, and hence the payment would be based on their use of the lighting. This may mean that the lights do not remain turned on all night and waste taxpayer money. Also it may mean that only those residents who use the lights pay for them rather than everyone in the community through taxes or any such collective charging schemes.

The pay-per-use charging mechanism could be provided through the agency of chip-and-pin technology that is available with most credit and debit cards. The lights connect to their COT (Cloud of Things) cloud via GPRS[1] and transmit information pertaining to such things as usage and bulb replacement. Other applications of a cloud of things would be for cars, houses, health monitoring equipment, household appliances, and offices.

Cloud Relationships

A common theme you will find with hybrid clouds is that its component clouds will need to share or integrate data in order to be able to port the cloud-based applications, or their services, from one component to another. Actually this need to share information is not specific only to hybrid clouds. A private or public cloud also has as its components other clouds that provide given tasks or services. But, for this to happen, there needs to be defined relationships between the clouds or between cloud cells. These relationships are considered as encapsulation, composition, and federation.

Encapsulation

Encapsulation is when an object contains or consists of another object. By encapsulation, one object is said to contain the other. Encapsulation minimizes your work because you can use a cookie-cutter approach with it. For example, a forest of eucalyptus trees could be described as a forest that encapsulates eucalyptus trees. From an engineering viewpoint, you only need to describe one tree and then describe the forest as an aggregate of that single type of tree.

Encapsulation is of two types: composition and aggregation. Our eucalyptus forest is an example of aggregation. Composition is when you have distinct objects that contribute to create an overall object, and not just one repeated object type as in the eucalyptus tree forest example. Suppose that you have to describe a car: it consists of four wheels, a steering, a bonnet, an engine, and so on. The car encapsulates these parts that, together, as a composite, make it a car. The car is a composition of its parts whereas the eucalyptus forest is an aggregation of eucalyptus trees. From a cloud computing perspective, one cloud can encapsulate another cloud or clouds. Hence, for our purposes, encapsulation is the composition or aggregation of cloud services. We discuss aggregation and composition in the following sections.

Aggregation

Aggregation is applicable to any cloud abstraction type. Figure 7 shows an aggregation for the SaaS cloud, where the SaaS cloud is made up of other SaaS components that

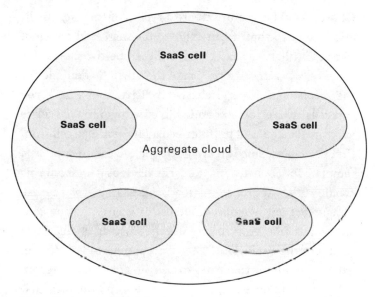

Figure 7   Aggregated SaaS cloud

can be described in similar terms with regard to the operating expenditure charges and the SLAs. So what use does aggregation have in practice? Let us re-visit our accountancy firm analogy. Suppose that our accountancy firm has an OLA with their IT department in providing accounts reconciliation through a SaaS cloud service. Suppose further that the accountancy firm has a surge in new clients—perhaps due to better marketing or a merger with another firm. The IT department now has increased demands placed on it that it cannot meet using the same

OLAs. It could therefore create a replica of their reconciliation cloud so that it can cater to the increased demand. The reconciliation SaaS cloud will then be two clouds (or cloud cells), each cell a replica of the other. So demand for the reconciliation service can be distributed across the two cells. The effort expended in creating a replica cell is very small compared to that needed in creating a cell from first principles, since an image of one cell can be used as a template for creating another. The obvious gain from this cookie-cutter approach, which is an example of the use of aggregation, is agility and cost efficiency. Let us consider another approach: suppose that instead of creating a replica of the SaaS cloud, the IT department identifies an external company that can provide the same type of reconciliation as its own cell, so it negotiates an SLA with that company for its cloud function to be the same as its own. This way they will have an SaaS cloud that encapsulates its own reconciliation cell together with the other company's cloud cell in order to meet the increased demand. The IT department could even go further and treat the other company's cloud cell as if it were its own so that any extra demand that its own cloud cell cannot meet would be sent to the other company's cell. This is known as "cloud-bursting," whereby one cloud bursts to another so that it can be elastic in meeting demand needs. Yet another use case for aggregation would be to have a cloud cell located in a different data center rather than the main center. The replica cell in the different data center can then be used for disaster recovery or business continuity. Both the primary and the secondary cells in the two data centers would be part of one SaaS cloud service that meets business continuity SLAs. Such a use case is especially useful when private clouds are involved. Last, IT could create a community cloud service that aggregates cells so that some cells that meet its requirements can be re-used or even shared with other community clouds provided that the cells are common to both community clouds.

In summary, aggregation has many use cases. Examples include (1) elasticity to meet user demand, (2) cloud-bursting across different clouds or service providers, (3) business continuity, and (4) re-usability or sharing cloud services that are common to different clouds—incidentally, the example here of a community cloud is applicable to other types of clouds too.

Composition

When a cloud is composed of one or more *distinct* clouds, composition is being used, as shown in Figure 8 where a composite cloud encapsulates five cells. A key benefit of composition is re-usability. For instance, a storage cell can be defined and used for one composite cloud and the same cell, or a replica created from its image, can be used in another composite cloud. This re-usability is predicated on standardization, so a standard storage cell definition

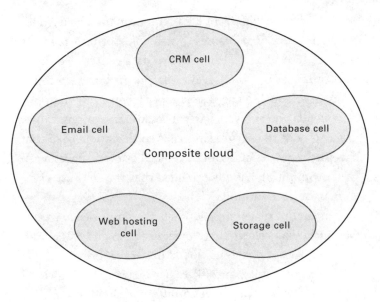

Figure 8 Cloud composition

with its own set of requirements, interfaces, functions, and management characteristics needs to be created. By management characteristics we mean:

1. updates and patches to the cloud cell,

2. upgrades to the cell's hardware,

3. upgrades to the cell's operating system and core applications that form part of the platform,

4. upgrades to the applications hosted on the cell, and

5. changes in the roadmap that define when upgrades and updates are to occur in future.

Any change to one characteristic of the standard cell will change that characteristic on all its replica cells. This makes managing changes much easier, although it does require extra testing because any change applied to a cell may be fine in one composite cloud but not in another. So all the composite clouds that encapsulate the replica cells derived from a given standard cell need to be tested in order to commit changes to the standard cell.

So standardization, re-usability, and manageability are key benefits of composition. Other benefits include agility in instantiating and provisioning clouds. That is to say, as you define a new cloud, you only need to decide what building blocks—in the form of cells—it should contain. And presto, you have a new cloud ready in minutes! Moreover with the higher level of abstraction provided by encapsulation, details such as how a cloud cell is built are not important. In creating the cloud cell, all you need to know is what a cloud cell does and not the details of how it is built and what it contains. The component cloud cells can be any type of abstraction or delivery model, and the same applies to the composite cloud. The composite cloud can be IaaS, PaaS, SaaS, INaaS, or BPaaS cloud, although higher levels of abstraction at SaaS and above are more likely when producing a composite cloud service.

Federation

Federation is a special type of composition. Cloud services provided by disparate clouds—usually from different cloud service providers—can be federated to create a composite cloud service. You may think of it as a "mash-up" of cloud services. The component cells of the federated cloud can be a mixture of your own cloud cells as well as a third-party's cloud cells. You can even have a federated cloud that is composed entirely of cells from third-party cloud service providers. This means that other than negotiating your SLAs and the prices, you do not have to go through the trouble of creating your own cloud or its cells. This approach assumes, of course, that the right cloud services are available from service providers. Apart from the benefit of rapidly creating and using your cloud, federation has another benefit, from a service provider's or broker's perspective. A cloud service broker can assemble a cloud that federates cloud services from a number of cloud service providers; can negotiate contracts, SLAs, and prices with them; and can dispatch the federated cloud service as an assemblage to you. As a cloud service consumer, you then do not have to negotiate terms and prices with all the other providers because you simply deal with the cloud service broker. Another benefit of federation is that you can ramp up your services, either by adding extra capacity to existing services in order to meet increased demand or by augmenting your service offering with extra services. You can do this because you have instant access to a global marketplace of cloud services. As a result, if you have a customer that suddenly needs resources or services that you do not have available as part of your current cloud service, you can simply purchase the service from the marketplace and add that service to your cloud service catalog as a cloud service broker or service provider. Yet another benefit is that you can use federation to ensure that one cell within your cloud will fork out work to another cell in order to balance the workload or to ensure failure safety. (Failure safety is when one cell takes over work from another if it were to fail, thus ensuring that a resilient service is provided.) Please note that federation is based on a major assumption: one cloud can integrate and interoperate with another. This "plug-and-play" feature, as afforded by interoperability, is discussed in more depth in chapter 10 on transitioning to the cloud.

Cloud Cells

A cloud cell is a cloud that provides a distinct, fundamental, function or service and further acts as a unit so that its service may be re-used by other clouds or cloud cells. Based on the cloud relationship principles discussed in the previous section, you can think of a cloud cell as a cloud that is encapsulated within another cloud. Examples would be a database cell that provides the services of a database server, a web server cell that hosts Internet sites, or an email server cell. In other words, the same type of cloud service does not need to be created for every cloud that needs it because you share the cell. You invest once in creating a cloud service—as a distinct cloud cell—and then leverage it so that other clouds can use it. (Of course, there are a lot of technicalities involved—how the cloud cell exposes its services to other cells, how it advertises its services to those cells, whether a service catalog is maintained by a controlling cell, and what common data models and formats ought to be used to pass information between the cells—but we won't delve into these details, since our purpose is to understand the main concepts.) This leverage provides cost efficiencies through re-usability. Thus having specific clouds that perform distinct functions that can be re-used by other clouds through the cloud relationships we assessed in the previous section can increase profits. This is the opposite of Gossen's First Law of Economics,[2] and can be thought of as providing an increasing marginal utility with usage. Likewise re-using cloud cells also increases agility in calling up a particular cloud function because you won't have to create it from scratch. The increased agility translates to a shorter time to market.

Figure 9 shows a cloud service—called a mother cloud—that consists of a number of cloud cells. The controller cell is optional, depending on the use, and its main purpose is to act as an orchestrator of services that the other cloud cells provide. Let us use a web service as an

Thus having specific clouds that perform distinct functions that can be re-used by other clouds through the cloud relationships we assessed in the previous section can increase profits. This is the opposite of Gossen's First Law of Economics, and can be thought of as providing an increasing marginal utility with usage.

example of a mother cloud, in which you could have the following cloud cells encapsulated: a web server cell, a database cell, a storage cell, and an SaaS cell that contains the business logic for the web service. A special form of cloud cell, used mainly within the IaaS and PaaS space, is the cloud gear. Cloud gears are specialist cloud cells that individually provide applications such as antivirus protection, hard disk encryption, public file sharing, and backup.

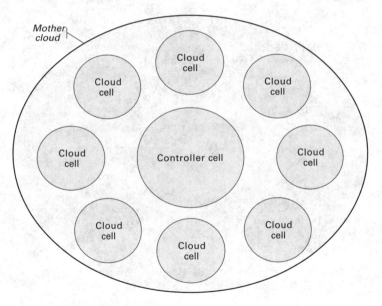

Figure 9 Clouds within clouds

Cloud Cell Patterns

The web service cloud we just considered follows a pattern. Like all web services, it has a database, some storage, business logic, and a web server. Those components, in essence, describe a pattern for a web service. Similarly, you can have numerous use cases: email service, inventory management service, order processing service, and audio streaming service are just a few examples. Each of these can be described as distinct cloud services comprised of cloud cells that provide distinct functions. Thus cloud patterns are implemented by cells, and they provide a template for a given cloud service or its use case.

Patterns are not new. In cloud computing they come to us from the field of object-oriented software and were first documented by the Gang of Four.[3] They described software patterns as objects that can be re-used to create a solution to a problem. They posited that a pattern has four essential elements:

Pattern name   An identity that creates a common vocabulary to invoke the pattern.

Problem statement   A description as to when and under what circumstances to apply the pattern.

Solution   Description of elements that make up the pattern (in our case, the names of the cloud cells), their

Table 3

Name	**Web server cloud service**
Problem	Host a customer facing website that uses business logic to respond to users in real time
Solution	Components: 1. Webserver cell: Contains Python, Apache HTTP server, and Node.js 2. Database cell: Contains PostgreSQL database 3. Storage cell: Provides storage for the other cells 4. Service bus cell: Provides connectivity with backend systems 5. Firewall cell: Virtual firewall implements a local demilitarized zone Relationships: Encapsulation—composition of above five cloud cells Interfaces: 1. Internal: Firewall → Webserver → (Database, Storage, and Service bus cells) 2. External: Users (via HTTP server), admins, and backend database (via Service bus)
Consequences	Price model: Consumption-based price model. Value models: User demand flexibility and location flexibility

relationships (we discussed these in detail in the previous section), and interfaces.

Consequences   Trade-offs and impact of using the pattern (in our case, the price and value model that would apply to the pattern).

Table 3 describes our web service example as a pattern using this Gang of Four framework.

The format of table 3 can be used to describe any number of cloud patterns that fulfill a particular use case. In chapters 6 through to 9 we show how various use case patterns can be used to create cloud service patterns. The components of the pattern then become distinct cloud cells.

CLOUD COMPUTING: A PARADIGM SHIFT?

Having read the two previous chapters, you know what cloud computing is and what it does. In this chapter we step back and ask some difficult questions. Why cloud computing? What does it give you? What is so special about cloud computing? And how will it affect you, your work, and our society? Just as Microsoft Windows became ubiquitous at home and work, and changed our lives, cloud computing represents a paradigm shift. This is because cloud computing is an enabling technology that bypasses many functions provided by your computer, the software installed on it, your workplace's IT and finance departments, businesses and government departments.

In this chapter we consider cloud computing's paradigm shift from three different viewpoints: (1) how it should affect you socially and personally, (2) how it will affect you in your work, and (3) how it will affect businesses.

Gartner's hype curve[1] shows that cloud computing is presently at its peak for inflated expectations. This chapter might be considered as providing a portent for those expectations whereas chapter 10, on transitioning to the cloud, will provide you with practical tools and frameworks to realize these paradigm shifts.

Social Paradigm Shift

How you spend your leisure and how you live, both at a personal and a societal level, are what we connote as social life. How that social life could be affected by cloud computing is the subject of this section. In order to consider that paradigm shift in your social life, let us examine the three types of clouds that would be the primary change agents: the societal or community cloud, the personal cloud, and the cloud of things.

Societal Clouds

A societal cloud is one that serves a group of people that have something in common. For instance, that common element could be defined by geography (along township, state, national, or international boundaries), hobbies (philatelists, numismatists, etc.), languages, or interests (trade unions, scouts, chambers of commerce, etc.). Your membership of the societal cloud would be defined by the common element you possess.

An international societal cloud could be defined for NATO, UNO, EU, and other such bodies. The citizens of countries belonging to an international body would then be members of that cloud. Common benefits or issues could be considered by the cloud members, which could host, for instance, discussion boards, instant messaging, storage of shared documents, and video conferencing. All this would be done in a secure environment. This is an example of a PaaS societal cloud.

Similarly a societal cloud could exist at a national level: for health care, training, politics, farming, and the like. The data collected could be de-personalized and aggregated to provide trend analyses. For example, in health care, the information collected with regard to a particular morbidity could be analyzed in terms of its concentration in particular areas, age groups, and social or income brackets, in real-time and an automated manner. The information could be made available freely to anyone researching the prevalence of morbidities in the aggregate. That information could be used to link multiple morbidities and their effects on members of a relevant societal cloud. Moreover the range and dispersion velocity of infections could be gathered from such a medical cloud to predict the spread of a disease across a country or region. This information can then be used to prepare the distribution of inoculations or medical resources.

A community cloud is one that provides a service to those who have a common interest. The common interest could be avocations such as farming, weather forecasting, trade bodies, banking, law and publishing. In a sense, with the Internet and various websites that cater to common interests, we already have Internet-based communities, known as social media. Converting these to societal clouds is more a case of using cloud elasticity and an appropriate price model. So the societal cloud is less of a paradigm shift from an individual's perspective. However, having a societal cloud that is a community cloud comprising of clouds (a societal cloud of clouds) enables member services to be defined in a unique and individual manner. Thus the societal cloud, at a high level, acts as a service broker for members belonging to a societal cloud and can tailor a society to suit an individual's background and interests.

Personal Clouds

A personal cloud is one that belongs to you for your use. You may already have come across such clouds in the form of Apple iCloud, Google Drive, or Microsoft OneDrive. These allow you to store files such as documents, eBooks, pictures, and music so that you may access those files from any device and any location. However, you should have a large choice in future with regard to various use cases[2] for a personal cloud. In general, we can consider a personal cloud in terms of the following three use case categories: leisure and well-being, finance, and shopping. Some of the examples cited may seem futuristic, but they demonstrate the use to which a personal cloud could be put to.

Personal Cloud for Leisure and Well-Being   The current plethora of storage clouds such as iCloud fall under this category. In the future, as storage becomes cheaper due to economies of scale, you should see video-streaming personal clouds that retain your collection of movies or video clips. This would be tantamount to having your own personal YouTube service.

Other personal clouds, such as a health wallet, could store information on the doctors you visited over a period of time, results of your health screenings, and the medical costs associated with the health checks. Various devices, such as your weight scale, pedometer, or blood pressure monitor, could be hooked up directly to your personal cloud to provide you with immediate alerts should your readings traverse the ideal thresholds. (While all those health devices hooked up might evoke an idea of an Internet, or cloud, of things, we classify such a cloud as a personal cloud rather than a cloud of things because such devices monitor you or are related to you and you alone.) A health service provider could aggregate everyone's health data, after de-personalizing it, to analyze the best fitness and health plans for you. Alternatively, the analytics could be sold to a health insurance company that would be able to predict the likely probability of health costs associated with someone in similar circumstances to you.

Another example of a personal cloud for leisure comes from motoring. A car could capture your driving profile and send it to your personal cloud. The information could be, for example, the average speed you drive at, the locations you drive through, your general driving style (aggressive or passive), and the number of accidents you have. Some cars already capture this type of information at present, but it is stored onboard rather than made available to you in your own personal cloud. A car insurance company could then use this information to tailor its car insurance offering to your driving profile. Yet another example is having smart street lights that sense your proximity and provide lighting to you on the basis of whether you have paid the local taxes or the road tax; those motorists who have not paid these taxes would not have the roads lit up for them unless they pay instantaneously, using technologies such as Near Field Communications (NFC), to have the lighting turned on. Of course, this assumes that a pact is not formed between the compliers and noncompliers to journey together in a group to foil the lighting scheme.

Personal Cloud for Finance A personal cloud that receives your bank statements as well as credit card transactions could provide you with a balance sheet and a budget on the fly. Then, at the end of the financial year when your personal finance cloud obtains income tax regulatory information from the government's INaaS cloud, this cloud could create an income tax statement for you automatically. If in the future a government agency were to allow the remittance of such electronic tax returns, your cloud would file the tax statement with the relevant government department upon your approval. Thus the chore of creating a tax return would be automated for most individuals, and they would not have the need to appoint an accountant. Another example of a personal finance cloud would be in terms of providing you with an integrated view of all your investments across various pension funds, IRA schemes, and brokerage accounts. This would enable you to assess, at a glance, what your investments' performance is over a given period at a moment's notice.

Personal Cloud for Shopping   Your personal shopping cloud would store your shopping preferences based on your shopping history across all stores. It would then analyze your buying pattern and alert you of what you need to buy in a timely manner by using predictive analytics. It could even scan discounts or offers at various stores, physical or electronic, to provide you with a purchasing choice. Further, it could manage your electronic wallet so that you could pay for the goods in a quick and easy way. A lot of work is currently being done by various companies on electronic payment schemes, and some of these payment schemes could be integrated to your personal cloud for shopping or to your electronic wallet.

Cloud of Things

A cloud of things is a cloud service that helps the management or use of a thing (a nonliving entity) by one or more living entities. (Those things are connected via the internet of things.) So, for example, you could have a cloud for your house. It would receive information from a number of sensors related to security, smoke, proximity, light, and other installed devices, and also automatically control other such things as curtains, fire alarms, lighting, and heating for you and other residents of that house. Moreover, depending on the room, each occupant of that room would have a personalized profile in terms of when curtains can be drawn or lighting turned on. Likewise, for your work environment, you could have a facilities cloud. Such a cloud is an example of a BPaaS because of the physical processes it manages automatically to benefit you, such as the drawing of curtains and monitoring of lighting. Another such example would be a meeting room cloud that keeps a logbook of the room's availability so that you can book the meeting room for a given period provided that it is available. The cloud could further inform various parties, such as security or catering, of its occupancy to enhance or ease the use of the meeting room. The meeting room cloud itself could belong to an aggregate cloud comprising of meeting room clouds, and those then could act in concert so that if a meeting room is unavailable at a certain time, you will receive a choice of suitable available rooms. This way you would have a selection of meeting rooms that fulfill your criteria in terms of room size or location, for instance. The meeting room aggregate cloud could in turn belong to the facility cloud, which itself would be a composite cloud. The section headed "Cloud Relationships" in the previous chapter can play a prominent role in the cloud of things because you could have various relationships—such as encapsulation, federation, composition and aggregation—between clouds of things in order to create other clouds of things.

Work Paradigm Shift

Two major trends are currently taking place in the workplace:

- Workstations replaced by zero or thin clients.

- Ubiquitous computing: use any device for work.

Workstations (laptops and desktops) are being replaced by machines that do not have applications installed on them. Such machines are known as zero clients if they have the operating system embedded on the silicon chips or thin clients if they require an operating system on disk. In order for a workstation not to have any applications installed on it, you need to use cloud-based applications to perform your work on the thin or zero client workstations. The clouds' hosting those applications can have varied deployment models: they can be private, public, community, or personal clouds, for instance. Generally, for productivity related applications such as Office or Email, you would use a public cloud service whereas for your own bespoke applications, you would use a private cloud service. But the applications do not necessarily have to be cloud based; they can be hosted on servers in the data center using traditional physical or virtual computing. As long as the application allows you access using a web browser, you should be able to use it regardless of the underlying technology used for hosting it. The benefit of a zero or thin client computing environment is that your company's IT department does not have to manage all those applications installed on a large number and variety of workstations. Instead, they manage just one application in the cloud or provide access to an application provided by a third-party's cloud service. Another benefit is that because the workstations do not contain any local disk or data storage mechanism, but instead use a cloud-based data store, the work information is stored at a central and, hopefully, more secure data store.

This means that if the workstation were to be lost or stolen, then the company's data would not be compromised. Indeed, in such a case, the zero or thin client workstation would be less expensive to replace as most of the application hosting, storage, and computing takes place elsewhere, in the cloud.

Ubiquitous computing started off with universities that needed to cater to a plethora of computing devices that students brought to the campus. Providing access to university-provided applications and information on various students' devices meant that a university's IT department needed to allow a secure way of allowing access to the university's resources on devices that the IT department did not manage or have any control over. As the technology developed, it became known as bring your own device (BYOD), which is currently being adopted by businesses to deliver IT to their employees. But ubiquitous computing is much more than BYOD; it means that you can compute and access corporate information from anywhere, not only from the campus or the workplace, by using any device and at any time. The onset of such a computing framework means that the IT department increasingly becomes a cloud service broker that maintains a service catalog of allowable cloud computing applications for an employee to use for work purposes. Those cloud-based applications then can be used from anywhere, at any time and on any device. Any data that need to be used or stored locally on the device are stored in a secure area within the device known as a sandbox. The sandbox is created when you become an employee and deleted when you leave the company. It stores the information so that only allowable applications can access it and further, the data are optionally encrypted.

Organizational and Business Paradigm Shift

Most businesses have an IT department that looks after central applications such as mail servers and web servers. The more business-related IT is performed locally by the business units or groups that deal directly with delivering a product or service to the customer. So you have a hub-and-spoke model wherein the centralized IT acts as a hub and the various business groups work autonomously in the periphery as spokes. If the central IT function is unaware of applications used by the various units or groups in the business, then those applications and their computers tend to be classified as shadow IT. If something were to go wrong with such an application or the computer hosting it, then there would be a problem in terms of supportability. A strong central IT department would refuse to support shadow IT whereas a weak one would support it at the cost of extra effort and money expended at learning about the system. In any case, shadow IT represents a potential security breach as well as an additional expense because of its nonstandard nature. For companies, shadow IT therefore represents a business risk.

As more applications become available via cloud computing, the business units are likely to increase their reliance on shadow IT because the spending threshold will be lowered, as figure 10 shows. Due to a greater level of abstraction provided by cloud computing, the skillset required to manage and support the shadow IT will diminish,

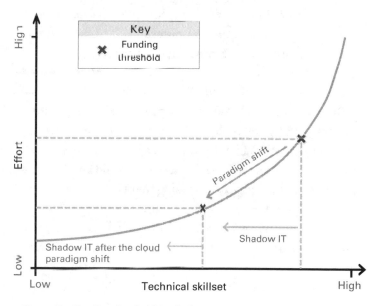

Figure 10   Funding threshold for shadow IT

and this will be a contributory factor in reducing shadow IT costs. Thus almost all the IT used in a company is bound to become cloud based. The central IT department, in order to survive, will need to evolve and become a cloud service broker. Doing this will ensure that the business departments will be enfranchised to work in a semi-autonomous centralized structure as far as IT is concerned. This will further ensure that shadow IT becomes mainstream IT and so will no longer be classified as shadow IT. As a cloud service broker, the central IT department would become a specialist branch of the purchasing department, since most of the IT and computational resources would be bought as services or used on a pay-as-you-go basis. The increased commoditization of IT due to cloud computing and related technologies will make this more possible as the technical skillset requirement to use and purchase IT diminishes, as shown in figure 10. The IT department's function will evolve to one that maintains cloud service contracts with cloud service providers, whose services would be listed and described in a cloud service catalog that the IT department would maintain.

How would the IT department then measure the value of a cloud service? How would it compare various pricing schemes from different cloud service providers in order to select the services to be made available via its cloud service catalog? We consider these questions in the next chapter where we discuss price and value models.

PRICE AND VALUE MODELS

Every undertaking has a cost and a benefit associated with it. Consuming cloud services is no different. This chapter considers the cost element of your using a cloud service and the price you pay for it after assessing various pricing regimes, known as price models. (Price models are also referred to as pricing models.) To offset the price you pay for the cloud service, you need to realize a commensurate benefit. That benefit is assessed by considering value models that can be related to cloud computing. Having an understanding of the price and value models will enable you to compare various cloud computing services in an objective manner. To help you in this regard, the chapter ends with a discussion of the various financial metrics that you would use for evaluating cloud services from a financial perspective.

Price Models

Price models provide a means of establishing the price that you pay in order to receive the value of a product or service. A cloud service provider will compute the costs of provisioning and operating a cloud service using a cost model. The cost model will then be converted into a price model. The type of price model selected will depend on the cloud service provider's business model, marketing strategy, and revenue expectations. In order to compare cloud services in an objective manner, it is important for you to know about the various types of price models.

Every price model starts its life as a cost model. The cost model is a financial model that the cloud service provider creates to find out how much money to outlay on a particular cloud service in creating it, operating it, and then refreshing it to newer technologies after three years. Three years is the usual life span of technology before it becomes outdated, and five years is generally the absolute maximum the cloud provider will have before replacing the technology. The cost model will include such factors as inflation, exchange rate variations (if applicable), depreciation, electricity costs (these can be significant because of the power and cooling required by a large number of servers), floor-space costs, software license costs, labor costs, and capital costs to buy and operate servers. Margin and a factor for risk are added to the sum of all the costs to arrive at a price. The price will have two characteristics: a nonrecurring and a recurring element. The nonrecurring element of the price is converted to a recurring element by amortizing the net present value into a series of recurring cash flows. (The mathematics for doing this is considered toward the end of this chapter under the heading of Net Present Value.) These cash flows are then added to the recurring element to arrive at a monthly price point for providing the service to you. This recurring price point is expressed as the price model and this price is used to sell and market the cloud service.

There are a variety of price models in existence. Broadly, let us categorize them as utility-, service-, performance-, and marketing-oriented models. Although cloud computing today mostly uses utility- and service-based price models, a wide range of models are considered because financial and business innovation is bound to catch up with technical innovation, thus enabling some of the less used models to enter the cloud computing domain in future. You may even choose to use or specify your own model in case you need to commission your own private, community, or hybrid cloud, after learning and evaluating all your options concerning the various price models discussed below.

Utility Price Models

Utility models are metered price models whereby your usage of the service is monitored and you pay accordingly.

Originating from the price plans that utility companies have adopted, they are characterized by regular payments, often monthly, to the cloud service provider. Three utility price models are discussed here: consumption, transaction, and subscription based price models.

Consumption-Based Price Model   The consumption price model is a commonly used model for IaaS and PaaS. You pay for the computing resources that you use, for example, amount of storage (in Megabytes or Gigabytes), computing or processing power (in terms of CPU cycles or number of processor cores used), and memory (in Megabytes or Gigabytes). An average consumption rate of these resources is computed over a day, week, or month and you pay for the average utilization. This is a rather crude model that does not scale well for SaaS, INaaS, or BPaaS, since for these resources you want to be charged in a meaningful way when it comes to how your business operates. For instance, for an INaaS service that provides you with the latest tax rules, you really ought not to care how many CPU cores or memory is used in delivering that information to you. But, for the cloud service provider, there could be other components that contribute to the cost of providing the service such as application licenses, data gathering, and maintenance costs. So for SaaS, INaaS, or BPaaS, other price models are more appropriate.

Transaction-Based Price Model Transaction-based pricing uses transactions, instead of computing resources, as the basis for pricing. The transactions can be business related, such as invoices processed for an invoicing BPaaS, data related for INaaS, or application related for SaaS. You can also have transaction-based pricing with IaaS and PaaS, for example, by using the bandwidth as an indicator of computing resource utilization; thus, a consumption-based price model can be converted to a transaction-based model by assessing the bandwidth used by each transaction.

The cost of a transaction is calculated by dividing the cost of providing a cloud service by the estimated transaction volume over a given period. This is then the unit transaction price. This price model is suitable under the following circumstances:

- Transaction volumes are known and predictable.

- Your business process can be defined clearly and can be measured in discrete units to represent a transaction.

- The transaction volume is tied to your cost drivers.

- From the cloud service provider's perspective: when business processes are standardized and driven by transactions.

Transaction pricing is most suitable for INaaS and BPaaS abstraction levels, and is equally suited to all cloud deployment models.

Subscription-Based Price Model   Similar to the all-you-can-eat model, the subscription price model is when you pay a price, usually monthly, in order to use a service. For example, when you subscribe to a magazine, you pay a regular fee regardless of whether you actually read all of it, some of it, or none of its articles. With the onset of web-based magazines or news portals, the content is refreshed quite often, so the content is not a fixed amount as with a paper magazine. Paying a subscription for such a service approaches the all-you-can-eat model as your capacity to consume becomes less than the rate of new content being produced. Sometimes there is a contractual period over which you are bound to pay the subscription. In cloud computing, for instance, you would have a monthly fee for computing resources that are allocated to you, and you would pay the monthly amount regardless of whether you used those allocated resources. Also you may have a notice period of three months such that, should you decide to no longer use the service, you would need to provide a notice three months beforehand. Subscription pricing can be used well for all cloud deployment models and abstraction levels.

Service Price Models

Service models use the benefit delivered to you, such as the SLA realized, risk transfer, or money saved, as the criteria for defining the price you pay for the cloud service. Broadly, the fixed price model is a risk transference model whereas the other two models discussed—volume and tiered—largely provide money and service benefits to you as a cloud user.

Fixed Price Model   The price that you pay for this service is fixed on a yearly, quarterly, or monthly basis. The fixed price can be made up of two components: recurring and nonrecurring prices. The latter is a one-off amount that you pay at the outset followed by recurring payments at regular intervals. The fixed price model is generally chosen when you have a clearly defined scope that is aligned to your short-term goals. Although this is used to transfer your risks related to delivery, people and quality, you will still own the risk of the service's scope by deciding how much of the service to use and to what extent. The risk transferal occurs through the SLAs that you define and agree with the cloud service provider. Fixed pricing can be used well for all cloud deployment models and abstraction levels.

Volume-Based Price Model   Volume can relate to the number of users, amount of storage space, speed of transactions (denoted as number of transactions per minute or hour), amount of bandwidth, or processing power utilized, for example. Any one of these parameters can be used as the basis for deciding the price you pay for the cloud service. Because volume varies over time, business cycle, or events such as a marketing drive, the price periodically changes. It is therefore imperative to define, calculate, and measure it. For instance, the price for a thin-client computing service where your employees use cloud services on a volume-based price model could be calculated on the basis of average users, peak users, allocated users, or concurrent users per day, or a combination of these. Similar considerations would apply to other parameters, should they be used in the volume pricing instead. Although volume pricing is most often used in IaaS and PaaS, it is just as suitable for the other abstraction levels.

Tiered Price Model   The tiered price model uses a tiered form of pricing that is based on SLAs, volume, or amount spent. It is similar to the tiers that airlines have for their membership levels that are determined by the amount you spend on travel with the airline. With cloud computing a similar form of tiered pricing can apply with greater discounts provided that you spend a certain amount each year. Alternatively, you could have tiers based on the SLAs such that the more stringent the SLAs, the more you pay. For example, there could be three SLA tiers and three different price tiers for them, with each SLA tier providing greater benefits to you. Or you could have the tiers based on volumetrics such as the number of users being served. That is, suppose your business requests a cloud service provider to provide storage to your employees such that they can store documents and access them from anywhere and from any computer. The storage provider could have three tiers for its pricing: for serving less than a hundred users, the price could be $5 per user per month; if your company needs storage for users between a hundred and a thousand in number, then the price could be $4 per month per user; and for more than a thousand users, the price could be $3 per month per user. These bands, or tiers, that define the prices for you on the basis of volume represent a tiered price model. And the basis for creating the tiers can be volume, SLAs, or the amount spent. Tiered pricing can be used for all cloud deployment models and abstraction levels.

Performance Price Models

Performance models are benchmark-based models that rely on key metrics, or benchmarks, to decide the price paid. Most performance models originate from employee remuneration or outsourcing related price strategies but can be applied to cloud computing, especially to a private or hybrid cloud service. Sometimes these models are used to align your business goals to those of your service provider's goals in order to create a true partnership.

Performance price models exhibit some common traits:

• They require a clearly defined output or metric that can be measured easily.

• The metric is often aligned to a business process or outcome with a demonstrable correlation to its impact.

We consider here the outcome, business-linked and gain-share price models as being within the category of performance models.

Outcome-Based Price Model   If your department wants to use cloud computing because it wants to reduce time to market (this being one of the seven value models), then you may want to negotiate a "bonus" payment to the cloud service provider that is linked to that outcome. Most outcomes use metrics that relate to cloud computing's value proposition, as expressed by the value models that we consider in the next section. There is a difference in psychology between the outcome-based model and some performance-related price models. With the former, you provide a bonus if an outcome is achieved, and with the latter, you penalize the provider if an SLA or benefit is not realized. Outcome-based models are often used with other models, usually fixed price models, in order to create a value culture based on rewards.

Business-Linked Price Model Whereas outcome-based models use metrics that measure the value of cloud computing, business-linked models measure the contribution that cloud computing makes to the KPIs that affect your business model. One of the challenges is linking the business outcome to the contribution made by cloud computing. Figure 11 shows a possible mapping between the objectives for using cloud computing, as per its value models described in figures 12 to 18, and the related business outcomes as expressed by business KPIs.

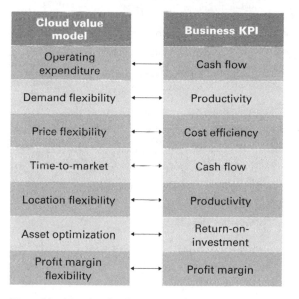

Figure 11 Mapping cloud computing objectives to business and financial KPIs

Gain-Share Price Model   The gain-share model has its roots in employees' remuneration schemes. The idea is that as the organization gains, it shares some of those gains with its employees. A typical gain-sharing organization measures its own performance and shares the profits with all its employees using a predetermined formula. The organization's actual performance is compared to its historical average (known as its standard or baseline performance) to determine the amount of the gain. In a cloud computing context, instead of having penalties should certain SLAs not be met, you reward the service provider by sharing your profits if the SLAs are exceeded. It is a different approach psychologically. However, you can combine the gain-share model with a penalty-based performance model to create a hybrid performance model.

Marketing Price Models

Certain price models are driven by marketing rather than performance. The key driver behind such models is to attract as much custom as possible and to then monetize it to create a profit. We discuss two such marketing led price models in this section.

Freemium Price Model   There are two types of freemium. One is where you try before you buy a more enhanced service, and the other type is where you get a free service but the advertisements provided to you make up for the service's price. This model is especially suited to SaaS because many software companies such as LinkedIn and Dropbox use it well. They offer a free version of their product that has limited functionality but provide you the option to pay for a premium service with extra features. The idea is to offer enough value to users in the free version in order to attract and retain them, and more value in the enhanced version to ensure that the users convert and maximize the service provider's revenue.

Razor-and-Blades Price Model   This pricing model relies on two components, a base component and a reusable component that the base component needs in order to deliver a service. It is akin to selling you razors cheaply, or even giving them away for free, and then making up for it from the prices of the consumable blades. Printers are another example; they are sold cheaply, but the price is made up from the printer ink supplies. In cloud computing, a device or an app that uses a cloud service may be given away, but the price may be made up from the data that is stored, analyzed, and presented by the cloud service. For example, you could have a blood pressure monitor that sends data automatically to a cloud service. The cloud service would then store and analyze the data, which it would use to alert you if a certain blood pressure level were traversed. The sensor could be provided for free or at a reduced price whereas you would pay for the use

In cloud computing, a device or an app that uses a cloud service may be given away, but the price may be made up from the data that is stored, analyzed, and presented by the cloud service.

of the cloud service that makes the sensor information meaningful to you. Another example of this is Amazon's kindle that can act as a window to a virtual storefront from which you could purchase a wide variety of goods. The kindle device is sold at a discounted rate, and is called a loss leader, but its value is made up from the increased sales revenue in the storefront that results from its use.

Hybrid Price Models

The utility, service, and performance price models discussed above are not mutually exclusive; they can be combined to produce hybrid price models. For instance, you could have a subscription-based system that utilizes a tiered approach. If the dollar spend per annum were to be at a certain level, then that level would decide the discount tier that would apply to you. One other approach would be to combine the risk transfer of the fixed model with the affordability of one of the utility price models to provide a fixed, monthly, price to the user such that they may consume as much of the service as they wish for that fixed monthly fee. This type of hybrid price model is quite common to many public cloud services such as Google docs and Microsoft Office 365. In fact this is a good pricing model for large or long-term services, especially if they need to be perfected over time. The hybrid price model can be applied successfully to all the cloud abstraction levels and deployment models.

Value Models

Value is generally something that a user derives when off-setting the benefits of a service by its cost. The sum total of the benefits can be thought of as those that you should specify or receive as part of the SLA. If you were to subtract the costs of cloud computing from the sum total of the benefits, you would arrive at a tangible sum that connotes value. Value, therefore, encompasses a cost–benefit analysis as it essentially computes as benefits minus costs.

In various disciplines, different types of value models exist. Just to name a few, there are the user expectancy value model, the place value model, and the customer value model. For our purposes in cloud computing, however, a value model is a standard pattern that defines value to you, as a user of cloud computing, and that is common to a number of users in similar situations. Considering the various benefits of cloud computing, let us examine seven cloud computing value models: (1) operating expense, (2) user demand flexibility, (3) price flexibility, (4) agility for time to market, (5) location flexibility, (6) asset optimization, and (7) profit margin as depicted by figures 12 to 18.

Operating Expense

In order to provide a computing service, your IT department would need to spend capital up-front in order to create and maintain the service. And for that service to remain within the bounds of your SLAs, the IT department would need to create extra capacity. All this capital expenditure represents an opportunity cost to you as the capital could have been employed elsewhere to pursue a business opportunity. Conversely, should the actual demand exceed the compute capacity that you have invested capital in, the extra demand will either not be met or will translate to degraded SLAs. The end result will be an opportunity loss to your business, since the unmet demand will cause loss of business to you. The operating expenditure model of cloud computing, as depicted by figure 12, uses elasticity to avoid opportunity costs and losses.

The upwardly slanting curve for computing capacity of figure 12 is based on two assumptions that are not mutually exclusive: that business demand will grow, and that more automation (i.e., elasticity and resources) will be made available over time via cloud computing.

User Demand Flexibility
Every product or service that your business provides to your customers has a life cycle that comprises of development, testing, launch, marketing and normal business usage. During each of these phases, differing demands are placed upon computing so that you will have periods consisting of peaks and troughs over the entire life cycle. To ensure that you meet all these demands, you will need to invest and disinvest in overprovisioning compute capacity. In any case, there will inevitably be periods where the demand will simply be unmet—especially during product

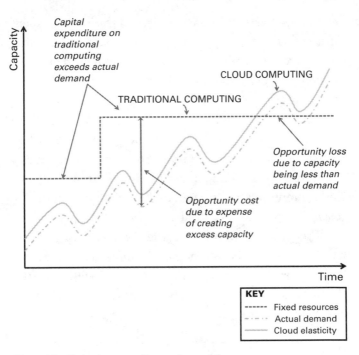

Figure 12 Operating expenditure value model

launches and marketing drives. The demand flexibility model of cloud computing, as depicted by figure 13, uses elasticity to ensure that the various demands on computing during your product's life cycle will be met on an as-needed basis. This means that your investment in computing, essentially the price you pay for computing services, flexes as your demand varies over your product's life cycle.

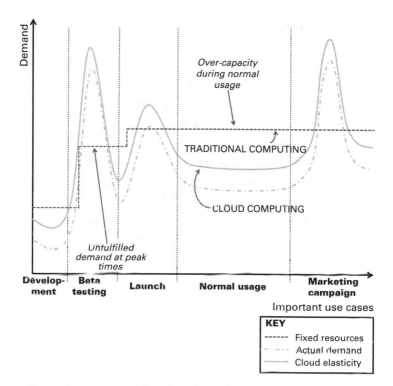

Figure 13 User demand flexibility value model

Price Flexibility

Over time the general trend in price for computing—regardless of whether it is traditional or cloud computing—is downward. This is because of newer technologies coming onto the scene at a fast pace and on a regular basis. Another contributing factor to the downward trend is the economies of scale resulting from the adoption of new technologies as the older ones reach obsolescence. Cloud computing gives you the ability to further introduce a step change to the downward price curve by using different price models as your needs and volume requirements change. So, for instance, at lower volumes, a consumption price model might be optimum for you, whereas a performance price model might be more suitable at higher volumes. Having the choice to change the price model, either using the same cloud service provider or moving to another, allows you to receive more value for money. Thus the price flexibility value model of cloud computing, as depicted in figure 14, uses different price models to lower computing costs over time as demand, volume, and circumstances change. Tiered and hybrid models are examples where the cloud service provider takes advantage of this to offer you greater discounts with increases in volume.

Time-to-Market Agility

The time-to-market value model of cloud computing, as depicted by figure 15, reduces your time to go to market by enabling you to transition from one computing environment to another at a faster pace. This is because you do not have to spend time commissioning computing infrastructure and environments beforehand, as with traditional computing. Rather, at a moment's notice, you can have any number of computing resources available to you to use in order to deploy your business application or service.

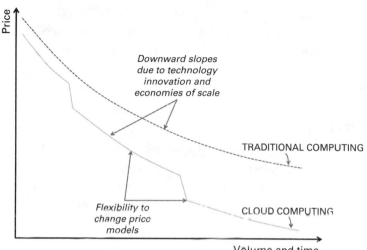

Figure 14   Price flexibility value model

Location Flexibility

The location flexibility value model of cloud computing, as depicted by figure 16, enables you to access your computing environment and work from any location due to the ubiquitous nature of computing. This flexibility increases your productivity and empowers you to have global reach.

Asset Optimization

The asset optimization value model of cloud computing, as depicted in figure 17, is similar to the demand flexibility value model of figure 13, except that the perspective is different. Figure 13 considers the unmet demand over a product life cycle resulting in loss of business, and figure 17 considers the extra investment you will need to make in order to have excess capacity in order to prevent loss of business. Or, rather, loss of reputation should your business be impeded due to lack of computing capacity. Additionally, when nearing end-of-life of your service, you are left with extra computing infrastructure that takes up needless space and so acts as a drain upon your cash flow. All this assumes that the asset life cycle that affects

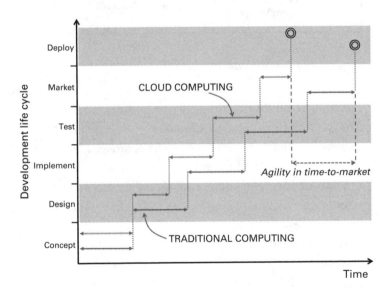

Figure 15   Time-to-market value model

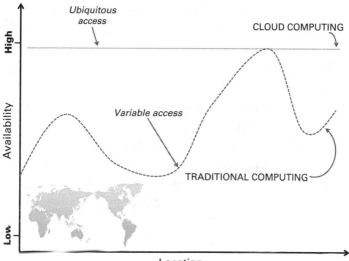

Figure 16 Location flexibility value model

investment follows the product life cycle. So you can optimize your assets through the use of cloud computing.

Profit Margin

When you produce any good or service, value-added costs
(including overheads) fall by about 25 percent every time
the cumulative volume, or your accumulated experience,
doubles. This results in a downward-sloping price curve
that increases your profit with experience, and this price
curve is known as the experience curve.[1] Cloud computing

is an evolutionary, though revolutionary in terms of its application, change to traditional computing as it draws on computing's cumulative experience. As such, it represents a shift in traditional computing's experience curve to the right. This moves the break-even point for using an outsourced cloud computing service, thus increasing your profit margin further. This is shown in figure 18, which is an adaptation of the BCG's experience curve of profit margin instead of costs. In fact one of cloud computing's value proposition is that it increases your profit margin

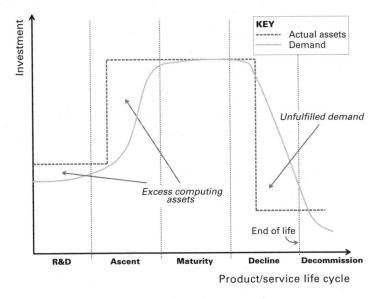

Figure 17 Asset optimization value model

more than traditional computing due to the experience curve effect.

Financial Metrics

How do you translate the value that cloud computing provides you into a meaningful financial measure? There are various financial yardsticks that can be used to assess the value proposition of a cloud service. Let us consider four

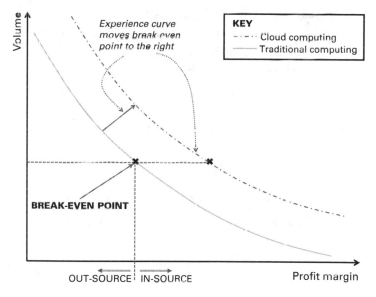

Figure 18   Profit margin value model

common financial metrics: payback method, net present value (NPV), return on investment (ROI), and time to market (TTM). There are other metrics that can be used as well, such as economic value added (EVA), return on assets (ROA), and return on equity (ROE). These latter metrics, however, are difficult to use when considering a single service, product, or project because they typically aggregate the computations at a corporate level and so rely on other factors such as the company's tax rate and its corporate KPIs. So we will not consider them further.

Payback Method

The payback method measures the time needed to recoup your investment in a product or service. A service that has a shorter payback period is deemed to be better than one that has a longer period, as in the following example:

- Suppose that you purchase a cloud service at $1,000 a month so that you can process invoices twice as fast as using your older system.

- Over a year, this comes to $12,000.

- Suppose that the old system processed $10,000 worth of invoices a month and the newer system will process $20,000 worth of invoices over a month.

- The value obtained is the difference between the old and new system, which is $10,000 per month because the new system is twice as fast.

- Per day, the value amounts to $333 worth of invoices assuming that a month has 30 days.

- This means that the new cloud service will pay for itself after 36 (equivalent to 12,000/333) days.

Usually the payback method is better suited for capital expenditure because you can depreciate it over a number of years. So the one year used in our example to arrive at an investment of $12,000 would need to be changed to encompass the years over which you can depreciate capital items. For operating expenditure, you would probably have a lock-in period or a contractual period with your cloud service provider, and it is this that would constitute the one year used in our calculation.

One of the shortcomings of the payback method is that it does not take into account the time value of money, which can have a substantial bearing on the investment calculation in periods of high interest rates or over long periods of time. To cover this, net present value (NPV) calculations are usually used.

Return on Investment
Whereas the payback method considers the time to recoup the investment, return on investment (ROI) uses the percentage of the investment amount that will be recouped.

ROI is widely used in the IT industry to assess capital investments. The formula for ROI is

ROI = (Gain from investment – Cost of investment) / (Cost of investment).

For our example of a new cloud service at $1,000 per month, the ROI would be computed as follows:

- The gain from the investment is $10,000 worth of extra invoices a month.

- The cost of the investment is $1,000 per month.

- Thus ROI = ($10,000 – $1,000)/$1,000 = 900%

Unadjusted ROI, as calculated in our example, assumes the present value for all gains and costs; thus the assumption is that all gains and costs are produced at the outset, which is not often the case. To adjust for this anomaly, usually an NPV calculation is performed that discounts the time value of money to get a more realistic value for ROI.

Net Present Value (NPV)
When you have multiple cash flows occurring on a regular basis, those cash flows are called a stream of cash flows. When regular streams of cash flows are equal in value, the

cash flows are known as annuities. Because of the effect of inflation and interest rates over time, a cash flow amount of $1,000 next month is worth more than the same amount paid to you fifty months later. To assess the present value to you of a series of cash flows, we use NPV calculations. The NPV of an investment is the present value of all future benefits, such as cash flows, generated by the investment, net of initial costs, discounted over intervals of time. For example, you are to receive $1,000 every year for three years and the interest rate is 10 percent. You would discount those cash

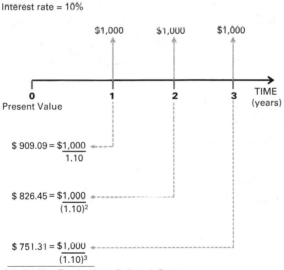

Interest rate = 10%

$1,000 $1,000 $1,000

0   1   2   3   TIME (years)
Present Value

$ 909.09 = $\dfrac{\$1,000}{1.10}$

$ 826.45 = $\dfrac{\$1,000}{(1.10)^2}$

$ 751.31 = $\dfrac{\$1,000}{(1.10)^3}$

$ 2,486.85 = Total value of all cash flows

Figure 19   Calculating NPV using cash flows

flows with the interest rate shown in figure 19, and then add the discounted values to obtain a net present value of $2,486.85. If you had made an initial investment of $2,000 in order to obtain those cash flows, then you would subtract that initial investment from the discounted cash flows to obtain an NPV of $486.85, and this would then represent a profit of 24.3 percent for your investment of $2,000.

Although NPV analysis is frequently used to justify capital expenditures, you can use it to perform a reverse calculation to come up with recurring expenditures as represented by that capital expenditure. Thus NPV provides a means for converting CapEx to OpEx, and vice versa. The benefits of using NPV analysis are the relative precision of the results due to the use of time value of money and the simplicity in the interpretation of its results: a positive NPV indicates a profitable investment. Another benefit of NPV is that opportunity costs are accounted for implicitly because of the use of a discount rate. Thus, if a projected rate of return is less than your hurdle rate, or your desired rate of return, then you would not make the investment. And of those candidate projects that do pass your hurdle rate, the one with the highest rate of return provides you with the optimum opportunity cost.

Returning to our invoice processing example, which had a cloud computing cost of $1,000 per month, let us suppose that the interest rate is 5 percent per annum and we decide to make use of the service for at least three years.

Those monthly outflows, as costs, can be represented as a capital expenditure using NPV analysis:

r = 5% ÷ 12 = 0.4167% (converted to a monthly rate)

N = 36 months

A = $1,000 (monthly amount)

FV = 0

$$PV = \sum_{k=0}^{N} \left(\frac{A}{(1+r)^k} \right) = \$ 33,365.70$$

The present value of using a cloud service by paying $1,000 per month for its use computes to $33,365 over three years. You then need to compare this amount with the amount that your IT department provides you with for creating your own computing platform. The lower value wins your investment time and money.

Time to Market (TTM)
Estimating the time when revenues will be obtained is another financial yardstick that can be used. For example, let us assume that using traditional computing it would take

you a year to go to market with a new offering that you are developing. With cloud computing, however, it could take you three months instead. So the TTM will be nine months sooner. And if you will earn $20,000 per month with the new system, then the earlier TTM would represent additional inflows of $180,000. Thus you can express TTM as time as well as its equivalent in monetary terms.

SECURITY AND GOVERNANCE

Security is holistic, not only for your organization's use of cloud services but also on behalf of the users sourcing those services, the applications associated with them, and the devices that allow access to the services. Additionally, we consider data integrity and privacy from an end-to-end perspective: from the user to the data center and back to the user. In this chapter we consider these issues and also legal and compliance issues related to data and its use. We extend this discussion to include data sovereignty and jurisdiction issues, since these are especially of concern to those of us who use cloud services. We conclude this chapter with a brief glossary of commonly used terms in the world of security; this should equip you with the knowledge to have a meaningful discussion with a cloud service provider.

What Is IT Security?

IT security protects the confidentiality, integrity, and availability of computer systems and the data they store or handle from unintended use. Confidentiality, integrity, and availability are often referred to as the "CIA triad." These attributes of security have evolved into the following six that are known as the "Parkerian hexad."

• *Confidentiality* Defines who can get what kind of information. For example, companies would be concerned about protecting their intellectual property; individuals would tend to be more concerned about unauthorized access to their financial or medical records.

• *Possession or control* Defines who and what systems possess the information or have control over its use.

• *Integrity* This refers to the information being correct or consistent with its intended use. Any unauthorized modification of data, whether deliberate or accidental, is a breach of data integrity.

• *Authenticity* This refers to the veracity of the information's origin or creation.

• *Availability* This refers to having access to the information in a timely manner, when it is required for its intended use.

- *Utility*   This refers to usefulness: having the information in a usable and useful manner so that it can be used as intended by the intended user.

Availability
One of cloud computing's characteristics is ubiquity, which adduces the availability of cloud computing resources. We therefore single out availability for more discussion.

Availability has multiple aspects:

1.   Will a service be available from any other location?

2.   How readily will it be available when you want to use it?

3.   Will there be certain times when it may not be available because of planned maintenance?

4.   If the cloud platforms hosting the service were to go down, how long would it take to recover?

5.   Once recovery is complete, will I have lost any data and, if so, how many hours' worth of data will it be?

The last two items are measured as metrics that are known as the recovery time objective (RTO) and the recovery point objective (RPO), respectively. Both metrics are expressed in terms of time, as hours, or minutes. Item 3 relates to downtime. It is usually expressed as a percentage that is calculated in the following manner.

% Availability = 100 * (Number of minutes downtime over a period) / (Overall minutes in the period)

The first two items in the list are usually not measured but should be defined in the contract with your cloud service provider. Availability metrics, however, should be measured and defined as SLAs that then form part of your contractual agreement with the cloud service provider.

Each of the CIA or Parkerian attributes can be given numeric values to denote its severity. For instance, 1 may represent low severity, 2 medium severity, and 3 high severity. Each of these severity levels may be delineated. Using availability as an example, 1 could represent RTO and RPO of 24 hours; 2 an RTO of 24 hours but RPO of 1 hour; 3 an RTO of 1 hour and RPO of zero hours. Suppose you need an RTO of 24 hours and an RPO of 2 hours, you would then specify an availability level of 2 as per our sample definition. This level would be the lowest level you could work with. Similarly, let us assume that your Confidentiality and Integrity requirements were expressed as levels 1 and 3, respectively. Hence you would express your security requirement in terms of the CIA triad as 1–3–2. You could instead choose to specify your security requirement using the Parkerian hexad and obtain 2–3–2–1–3–1 in reference to CPIAAU as an example.

Enforcing Security

An IT security breach can be described in terms of the six attributes of the Parkerian Hexad. Those attributes possess two characteristics. They are atomic and non-overlapping—atomic because they cannot be broken down into further constituents and non-overlapping because they refer to unique aspects of information security. Our definition of IT security raises a number of questions: Who decides what is intended, or nonmalicious, use? How do data get categorized as requiring more or less secure use? Who or what uses the data and why are the data accessed? What systems need to process the data? Where and how are the data stored and used by these systems? Let us attempt to address these questions from a best-practice perspective.

For our purposes, a cloud service user can be a person, a process or application, or a system such as a computing device. Support staff, when called to help resolve an issue, are also classified as a user. If we were to follow the data trail, the data would originate from a *user*, pass over a *network* to reach a *computing system* that hosts *software*, which processes the data and stores it in a *storage device*, such as a solid state disk, and that data gets backed up onto a *backup device* and finally, after a period of time, gets archived in an *archival system*. The elements that handle the data, as given in italics, are user, computing system, software, storage device, backup device, and archival system. And this entire

If we were to follow the data trail, the data would originate from a *user*, pass over a *network* to reach a *computing system* that hosts *software*, which processes the data and stores it in a *storage device*, such as a solid state disk, and that data gets backed up onto a *backup device* and finally, after a period of time, gets archived in an *archival system*.

data journey needs to be secure from the perspective of the user. The user's needs for privacy, data integrity, and security delineate the other elements' security measures.

To illustrate the security planning involved during this data journey, let us consider archival. The archival system needs to store data in a secure manner so that unauthorized users do not have access to the data, and that the encrypted information would not be comprehensible to them if they did obtain access. The backup process similarly ought to back up the data in a secure manner. The transfer of data from backup to archival system must further be kept secure. Thus each of the elements in the data journey described must share the same security characteristic in terms of the CIA triad or the Parkerian hexad in alignment with the user's requirements. Moreover data transiting from one element to another need to be secured, so the channels that enable such data transfers must also be made secure.

Security Containers

All those elements within the cloud computing environment that share the same security characteristics for a particular user can have a common security boundary. The computing elements that reside within that boundary trust each other. The environment formed as a result of that security boundary is called a security container. Thus, rather than define security boundaries for each elements that have touch points with data, segmentation is generally used to create a container, which then contains the elements that share the same security attributes. This segmentation usually takes place at the network layer, since the network is the mode of transport for information. Thus virtual networks are created that exist on a physical network and each container uses virtual networks inside it so that other containers (outsiders) cannot have access to its internal data. In order to enter a particular container, three security procedures are normally used: identification, authentication, and authorization.

Identification ascertains the user's identity. The user can be a person, application, system, or "thing" that wishes to connect to the cloud or its security container.

Authentication establishes whether the user is a legitimate user. Usually authentication is based on what you have or what you know. An example of what the user has would be a smart card, finger print, or voice biometrics, while an example of what the user knows would be a password or a PIN (personal identification number).[1] Authentication takes place once a user's identity has been established.

Authorization establishes the tasks that an authenticated user is allowed to perform. The rights given to an authenticated user depend on the role that the user has within the cloud computing environment. Authorization always takes place after a user has been authenticated.

Thus identification asks "who are you," authentication asks "are you who you say you are," and authorization asks "what are you allowed to do within the cloud computing environment."

One of the common concerns that users of cloud computing have is that the data stored in the cloud may end up being stored in a country that differs from the one where the user resides. Such concerns relate to the legal or regulatory jurisdiction of the data stored. Should the data be compromised, then which country's laws or data protection mechanism should apply? This is a valid concern because the elastic characteristic of cloud computing can indeed move computing resources, including data storage, from one place to another. Alternatively, it could be a case that the cloud is hosted in one country but its users come from another. In order to address this challenge, I propose the use of security containers that are defined in terms of their jurisdictional characteristics in addition to the CIA or Parkerian ones. This would mean that the data segregation takes place not in the data center but across any part of the world from where the cloud service is provided; by implication, this entails that the security container be created using virtual wide area networks rather than virtual local area networks. Thus we could add the letter J to the CIA or Parkerian attributes for "jurisdiction" as defined by legal/regulatory requirements.

Monitoring

The first defense mechanism that is employed to deter security breaches is a firewall. A number of firewalls would be placed at the boundary of every security container. The cloud itself, being a security container, will therefore have an outer firewall. Where you have containers within containers, which is not uncommon, then you would have firewall after firewall to traverse if you followed the data flow. The firewall will contain rules that tell it what traffic to allow through and what traffic to block. You can be alerted if someone tries to enter a security container and is blocked by the firewall. The alert can be an email or an entry in a log file that can be monitored. However, a security system will have a number of components such as firewalls, user authentication and identification, intrusion detection and prevention, and user-based security such as anti-virus and anti-malware tools. Such a system, if properly configured, will generate logs that will keep track of users, services provided to the users, and data. Reviewing the log files by humans is not possible, since the logs grow to a large size very quickly. As such, software is used to analyze the server and firewall logs, as a first step in monitoring, in order to detect any suspicious activity.

The second line of defense is at the user authentication and identification stage. If a number of failed attempts are made to log in as someone or to a particular service, then the monitoring tools ought to alert the cloud system administrator of this. If the tools are automated, then they may deny further log-ins on that account or to that service by the username concerned. Additionally, certain traffic can be deduced to be suspect because it is trying to use a service that is not allowed for a particular user, or it is trying to retrieve data that would normally not be needed by the user. All such traffic can be analyzed and reported by software that is known as intrusion detection system (IDS).

The third line of defense is at the client side. The client devices themselves need to be protected against malicious attacks so that user log-in details may not be compromised in order to access cloud services. Usually this takes the form of anti-malware (included in this is anti-virus, anti-spoofing, personal firewalls, and blocking of tracking cookies[2]) that is installed on the client device that you use to access cloud services. Mostly such end-user client devices are outside the scope of a cloud service provider to monitor or configure. It is this, then, that becomes the weak link in the security chain. However, with thin or zero-client computing, this weak link should become irrelevant as the client device should have a centrally managed operating system.

Data Integrity

Say you place a letter that contains some important information in a safe; you then bury the safe somewhere and do not let anyone know about it. That, in information security (or IT security) terms, is obscurity—not security. But, if you were to place the letter in a safe and send it to the letter's addressee so that only that recipient can read the letter, then you are sending the information in a secure manner. Now, if the safe were to be intercepted and breached, then three scenarios may arise: (1) the interceptor has possession or control of the letter and can withhold it from you or the recipient, (2) the interceptor can read the letter and use its contents to further that interceptor's own purpose (e.g., impersonate you by stealing your identity or hack into your computer systems), or (3) the interceptor could replace the letter and send it to the recipient so that false information is received. Data integrity aims to secure the communication channel or the data sent across it in order to ensure that none of these three scenarios occur.

For maximum data integrity, three elements are considered in securing the flow of data from one person (or user) to another. The end-points need to be secure—that is, the sender and recipient of the data need to be authenticated so that you know that they are the ones for whom the data is meant; the channel over which the information is sent needs to be secure so that other parties may not easily eavesdrop or false data may not be sent instead by others (man-in-the-middle attack); the data needs to be encrypted so that the data cannot be readily read by a third party. These three elements are not mutually exclusive, and you will often find a combination of these three measures used for ensuring data integrity.

So we need to consider how to ensure data integrity through the use of encryption, how to use checksums to verify your data's integrity, and finally the scope for data integrity in terms of a holistic data loss prevention strategy.

Encryption

To secure the channel, or network, that you use when transmitting sensitive data, you need to encrypt the channel. The data sent through that channel can also be encrypted, but often this is not the case. Channels are encrypted by the use of certificates that allow the sender and receiver to communicate over a trusted channel. Such an encrypted channel is known as a Secure Socket Layer (SSL) connection. When two parties need to communicate over a secure channel, the following handshake protocol is used:

• sending device uses public–private encryption keys to encrypt the channel,

• best-practice is to use valid certificates (these contain the public key) signed by a trusted certificate authority (CA) in order to kick-start the process,

• both parties agree upon the cryptographic protocols to be used, and

- they negotiate a shared secret (the private key) to use,

- receiving device uses the public–private encryption keys to decrypt the channel.

Once the handshake is completed between peers, both parties start to communicate in a secured fashion using the negotiated encryption algorithm and cryptographic keys. This secure channel protects them against any eavesdropping or man-in-the-middle attacks.

The concept for data encryption is similar except that the data are encrypted by the cloud service and decrypted by your application, or vice versa depending on direction of data flow. So the applications, instead of the web server or web browser, perform the encryption for data.

Checksums

To establish the veracity of data you receive, certain algorithms are used to compute checksums on the data. The data and the checksum then need to be corroborated by the receiver in order to trust the data received. Let us suppose, for example, that you were to send me a letter. Separately, you could also send me some information such as "the letter has 251 words, of which there are 105 nouns, 81 adjectives, and the rest are pronouns or verbs; it also contains 45 sentences and 5 paragraphs." This information describing the letter you sent me is akin to a checksum.

Various algorithms are used to compute checksums automatically and on the fly so that the receiving party can ensure the accuracy of the information that has been sent. Checksums principally guard against man-in-the-middle attacks to ensure that retrieved (from disk storage) or received (from a transmitting device) data have not been compromised after having been intercepted. A secondary use is to ensure that the received data has not been corrupted due to lossy or noisy channels of communication such as wireless networks.

Data Loss Prevention

Data loss prevention refers to systems that discover, identify, monitor, manage, and protect data that are in use, in motion, or at rest—wherever the data are stored and used. Usually, data loss prevention is used for confidential or private data. Figure 20 shows the three states of data that define the scope for data loss prevention together with common examples of places where data in each state can be found. These three states encompass the entire life cycle of the data: creation, transmission, usage, storage, archival, and final destruction. Thus data-at-rest refers to inactive or semi-active data that are stored physically in any digital form; data-in-motion is fluid data that are being transported from one end-point to another; data-in-use is active data that are in constant use.

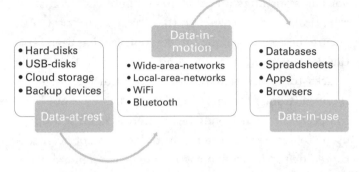

Figure 20   Three states of data

As a user of cloud services, you should ensure that data loss is prevented during the entire life cycle of the data as defined by the three states of figure 20. This is done by employing tools such as encryption (to secure the data), checksums (to verify the data's integrity), monitoring (to know who has accessed what data), and management (to ensure that stale or unused data is destroyed within time-bound limits.)

Data Privacy

We regard privacy as applicable to information that identifies a person. This is generally known as personally identifiable data (PID) or personally identifiable information (PII). The NIST defines PII as any information about an individual that includes:

(1) any information that can be used to distinguish or trace an individual's identity, such as name, social security number, date and place of birth, mother's maiden name, or biometric records;

(2) any other information that is linked or linkable to an individual, such as medical, educational, financial, and employment information.[3]

Most countries have data protection laws in place to ensure that such data do not fall into the hands of unauthorized parties. Most such laws include data retention directives, for example: "providers of services should erase or anonymize the traffic data processed when no longer needed." This is an example of a good directive that most cloud service providers ought to comply with. However, the same law in most countries often has some directives that are just impractical to follow—especially those related to cookies—to the extent that no website today complies, or attempts to comply, with such directives. As a result data protection laws have been discredited somewhat and have not been treated as seriously as warranted by many service providers.

Data privacy is closely tied to data integrity. In order to ensure that your data remain private, you need to ensure that its retention and transmission is implemented with data integrity tools. Security is usually enforced with intrusion detection, intrusion prevention, use of firewalls, antivirus, and anti-malware tools. But if these are breached, as they so often are, then your private data would be readily available had you not encrypted it. You can encrypt data that has been stored on your hard drive, disks, or cloud storage; this is known as encrypting "data at rest." Thus data that has been obtained as a result of a security breach would then not be accessible due to the data's being encrypted. In addition to "data at rest" encryption, you can encrypt data that you send to others via email, file-sharing products such as Dropbox, or to your own cloud storage. This encryption protects data during transit, and it ensures that any interception of the data while it is being transmitted from one place to another would be prevented from being read by an interceptor.

However, encryption as well as other measures protect your data from only nongovernment actors. Some governments can, and do, ensure that backdoors are in place at a number of strategic locations so that they can access your data readily. Examples of strategic locations can be the firmware[4] of devices that (1) route the data—such as routers, VOIP[5] servers and modems; (2) store the data—such as the hard-disks; (3) provide data security—such as firewalls and intrusion detection; and (4) encrypt the data. These backdoors are usually implanted in the firmware of the devices so that no user or software can be aware of their existence let alone be able to guard against them. With the onset of the Internet of Things, the ubiquity of the backdoors should increase markedly since the "Things" that are connected to the Internet could have such backdoors in their firmware. However, at present, only a select few governments (I would guess just two or three) have this capability. One way that you could ensure that your "Internet of Things" device has a relatively small chance of being compromised by such backdoors is to insist that its firmware is open source. This relies on software developers and engineers to have noticed the existence of such backdoors should they have examined the source code of the firmware.

Legal and Compliance Issues

Cloud computing, like law, is a tool that ought to be used to help the good and protect them from the bad. Unfortunately, in real life, complexities arise and things do not always work out that way. One of the reasons is that technology (cloud computing, its latest innovation, is a good example of this) changes very fast in comparison to laws and the legal framework. This gives an opportunity for early adopters to interpret or bypass the spirit of the law where a vacuum exists in the letter of the law. To some extent, this can be for the greater good as it does not stifle innovation. Yet security breaches and exploitation of users result from such an environment. A balance therefore needs to be struck. A large part of the solution is to educate the users as well as the legal community in terms of the information that can be collected, analyzed, and used as a result of the progress in technology. Another aspect is to provide a broad framework for information use for technological innovation to conform to. This has greater traction with industrial bodies than governments. Industrial bodies—especially the financial industry—that define regulations in order to protect participants and consumers have a number of regulations. Compliance with a variety of regulations, whether they be national, regional, or international, currently does not pose too much of a challenge to cloud computing. However, over time, should the various countries and regions come up with their own regulations for each industry sector, then there could be chaos. Then a particular cloud service would need to comply with a large variety of laws and regulations, some of which may even conflict. Greater cooperation and standardization across industry bodies and governments is therefore needed. An example is MiFID (Markets in Financial Instruments Directive), a law in the European Union that regulates investment services in order to increase competition and consumer protection. The main challenge with regulations, however, is jurisdiction. What regulation or law should a cloud service conform to if it is provided by a company established in country A, its users are principally from country B, its data are stored in country C, while the cloud service itself is hosted in country D? In such cases you should take care in specifying the legal and regulatory jurisdiction of a cloud service before buying and using it. In particular, you need to be aware of who would see the data, what systems would handle it, which applications would use it, and then establish the legal jurisdiction of those people, infrastructure, and applications.

Data Sovereignty

Tied closely to legal jurisdiction is the jurisdiction of ownership of the data. If a number of people have been involved in creating data, or if the data are consumed by a number of parties, then who owns the data? What if the data had been manipulated by intermediate systems or cloud services, who would own the data then? Would it be the original creator of the data, the intermediaries that augmented the data or the end user of that data? And what if all those actors were in different countries that had different data protection and ownership laws? These are some of the quandaries that face data sovereignty issues, and they relate acutely to cloud computing because of its characteristic of ubiquitous access. You should therefore ensure that you have a data ownership agreement with your cloud service provider that, additionally, considers the legal jurisdiction for redress in the event that the agreement is breached.

The Holistic Nature of Security

Security is holistic and is not just technology's concern or the cloud service provider's concern; it is everyone's concern. Security covers physical access to the computing devices, the divulgence of your passwords to others (either knowingly or unknowingly), and, of course, the enforcement of a security policy. Security, then, is a shared responsibility between you and the cloud service provider. The service provider is normally responsible for security in the infrastructure up through the interface point between your application and its hosting environment in the cloud. You, however, are responsible for security with respect to interfacing with the cloud environment, and importantly, within the application that uses that cloud environment. Let us consider as an example an application that you might want to install on Amazon's cloud service, known as Amazon Web Services (AWS). Amazon provides a virtual firewall that is called a Security Group that ONLY allows traffic that is specific to your application to flow. The best-practice with respect to Security Groups is to use them in containers, with each container having its own virtual machine hosting a specific application. This ensures that only traffic appropriate for that application instance and its virtual machine is allowed access. For example, web server virtual machines are configured to allow web traffic by opening a TCP/IP port 80 while a database server ought to be in a Security Group that blocks web traffic, meaning traffic that comes through on port 80. This measure guards against attacks to your database from the outside world using web traffic. Thus the onus is on you, as the installer of your application (this application, in our example, comprises of web and database servers) to ensure that it is securely installed in your private cloud environment.

Often the weakest link in any secure system is the human being. It is up to us humans, the users of technology, to ensure that the computing systems we use remain secure by taking a number of precautionary measures:

- guarding our passwords,

- ensuring that anti-malware (virus, phishing, cookie management, etc.) is in place and is updated regularly,

- intrusion detection and prevention using personal and router firewalls is running, and

- generally not opening emails or visiting websites that look suspicious.

These measures should ensure that the devices that you use to access your cloud services remain secure and are not compromised. Further, you need to ensure that any data you transmit to your cloud is encrypted so that it may not be read even if it is intercepted by a third party. There is very little technology can do if you, as the user of that technology, do not use it in a secure manner!

Common Security Terms

This section provides some commonly used terms in security. Knowing these terms and what they mean will equip you with the knowledge to ensure that your systems and data are secure when using cloud services.

Access control   Ensures that access to services is only granted to entitled users.

Backdoor   Code installed to give an attacker easier access to a system by bypassing security mechanisms that are in place.

Biometrics   The use of a user's physical characteristics in order to determine access to a system or service.

Business continuity plan   A plan that takes measures to ensure that a business remains operational in the face of a disaster, an emergency, security breach, or attack.

Checksum   A value computed using the data that is stored or transmitted; it is used to verify the retrieved or received data respectively.

Confidentiality   Ensures that information is disclosed only to those who are authorized to view it.

Custodian   The user or application that is currently using or manipulating the data, and so is temporarily taking responsibility for it.

Decryption   The process of transforming an encrypted message into its original plaintext.

Digest authentication   Ensures that a client application or user can provide proof that they have a password to use the system or service.

DMZ   A De-Militarized Zone (DMZ) is a perimeter network area that sits between an organization's internal network and an external network, usually the Internet. It forms part of a layered security model in which network segmentation is used to ensure the transit of data between a secure layer and an insecure one.

Encryption   Cryptographic transformation of data (called "plaintext") into a form (called "cipher text") that conceals the data's original meaning to prevent it from being known or used.

Escrow passwords   Passwords that are written down and stored in a secure location (e.g.,, a safe or an encrypted USB drive) that are used by emergency personnel when privileged personnel are unavailable.

False rejects   When an authentication system fails to recognize a valid user.

Firewall   A logical or physical discontinuity in a network to prevent unauthorized access to data or resources.

Fragmentation   The process of storing a data file in several "chunks" or fragments rather than in a single contiguous sequence of bits in one place on the storage medium.

Fuzzing   Regression testing that generates out-of-specification input for an application in order to find its security vulnerabilities.

Integrity   Ensures that data have not been changed accidentally or deliberately, and that data are accurate and complete at the point of use.

Integrity star property   Approach whereby a user cannot read data of a lower integrity level than their own.

Intrusion detection and prevention   Identifies and prevents security breaches, which include intrusions (attacks from outside the organization) and misuse (attacks from within the organization). This is usually performed at the inside and outside boundaries of a DMZ.

Lattice techniques   Uses security designations to determine access to different types of information.

Malware   General term used to denote viruses, worms, trojans, and any form of unauthorized software; malware stands for "malicious software."

Masquerade attack   A type of attack in which an illegitimate user or application poses as a legitimate one.

Nonrepudiation   System to prove that a specific user and only that specific user sent a message and that it hasn't been modified.

Penetration   Gaining unauthorized logical access to sensitive data by circumventing a system's protections.

Pharming   Technique whereby a user's session redirected to a masquerading website or application.

Plaintext   Data before being encrypted into ciphertext or data that have been decrypted.

Proprietary information   Information that belongs to an organization and gives it the ability to do business. This includes customer lists, technical data, costs, and trade secrets.

Risk   The security risk can be computed as the product of the threat level and vulnerability level in order to quantify the likelihood of a security breach.

Threat assessment   The identification of types of threats that an organization might be exposed to.

Trojans or implants   Malware that is disguised as benign programs or applications.

User   A person, organizational entity, or automated process that accesses a system, whether authorized to do so or not.

Virus   A hidden, self-replicating section of computer software that usually contains malicious logic and propagates by infecting another program or application.

Worm A program that can run independently and propagate a complete working version of itself onto other computers on a network; it may consume computer resources destructively.

Zombie A computer that has been compromised by malware.

USE CASE PATTERN #1: IAAS AND PAAS

In the first two chapters, we discussed abstraction levels when discussing service models. In this chapter, we build on that discussion by considering the general uses of the IaaS and PaaS abstraction types, their pros and cons, and the price models most suited for them. In particular, we will consider:

• various business use cases that employ the IaaS and PaaS deployment models,

• SWOT analysis of the use cases, and

• questions to ask when buying IaaS and PaaS based cloud services.

Typically, a use case is used to define requirements and the sequence of interactions in order to effect a solution in the form of a service, function, or application. When commonality is detected between use cases that can be implemented using a distinct solution, then it is called a *use case pattern*. These use case patterns can generally be implemented using micro-services. When standardized and implemented in the cloud, we shall refer to them as *cloud cells*. Thus cloud cells implement use case patterns. We consider use case patterns for IaaS and PaaS in this chapter. Subsequent chapters cover the other cloud deployment models.

In conjunction with this chapter, you may wish to refer to the checklist provided in the chapter "Transitioning to the Cloud" that considers many of the questions you would ask, in a nutshell, when considering cloud computing. Please bear in mind that commercial examples provided in this chapter to illustrate various use cases are not comprehensive and are for illustrative purposes only.

Use Cases for IaaS and PaaS

In IT, infrastructure encompasses the computing devices that you use to run software as well as all the other supporting components for those computing devices. The computing device can be a smart phone, a tablet such as an iPad, a laptop, or a desktop computer. Take email as an example. In order to deliver emails to your computing device, a mail server is employed that sits in a data center. This mail server receives mail from the Internet and routes it to you via the local area network; it is an application that is hosted on a computing device called a server. The server serves client devices, such as your tablet or laptop, and this architecture is referred to as the client–server model. A network is needed to connect the server to its clients, and so the network also is part of the IT infrastructure as are the network devices such as firewalls and switches. Your emails are stored on disks in the data center. These disks are linked in arrays, and they need to be very fast in order to serve a number of email accounts at any one time. Usually the disk arrays are configured as Storage Area Network (SAN) or as Network Attached Storage (NAS) devices. For our purposes, it is not important to examine these devices further, so we will refer to them generally as storage devices. These too form part of the IT infrastructure. Thus IT infrastructure is comprised of end-user computing devices (laptops, smart phones, tablets, etc.), the servers in the data center that serve those end-user devices, and the storage, the network, and networking devices. Applications that perform mundane, day-to-day tasks, such as routing emails, are also part of IT infrastructure. These applications sit just above the operating system and below the software layer. They form the integration layer between the operating system and the other applications, and are considered the "glue" between applications by enabling communication and management of data among them; these integration applications are commonly categorized as middleware and are, as such, components of the IT infrastructure.

In cloud computing, the IT infrastructure is grouped into two distinct granularities. All the physical devices such as the server, network, storage, and computing device, are denoted "infrastructure." When the servers and computing devices are combined with their operating system and middleware, they are referred to as "platform." Hence both infrastructure as a service (IaaS) and platform as a service (PaaS) are part of the IT infrastructure stack. Below we consider some of the principal use cases for both of these abstraction levels. Remember, you can build a SaaS service by using PaaS and writing an application on it that has multi-tenancy. Similarly you can build upon PaaS and SaaS by creating an information dissemination service (INaaS) or a business process service (BPaaS), with the addition of information or business processes, respectively. In the same manner, PaaS builds upon IaaS through the addition of an operating system and middleware to the hardware.

Figure 21 shows the principal use cases for infrastructure as a service. Some of these cases are examined in this chapter. In reading about these use cases, you will find a common thread connecting them: IaaS and PaaS are ideal

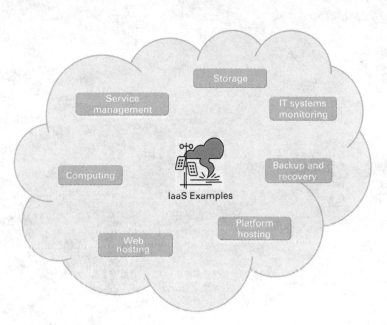

Figure 21 Use cases for infrastructure as a service

for tasks that require computing-intensive workloads, storage, backup (this is actually storage in a different place or medium), hosting of applications, or services like web hosting where there can be large variations in the number of users and where generic, background, services are needed. This pattern for IaaS and PaaS is suited to a variety of user categories, from established universities that can benefit from a community cloud to a startup that needs to go to market quickly using agile methods.

In cloud computing, the IT infrastructure is grouped into two distinct granularities. All the physical devices such as the server, network, storage, and computing device, are denoted "infrastructure." When the servers and computing devices are combined with their operating system and middleware, they are referred to as "platform."

Computing

Let us suppose that a university department has a problem, consisting of numerous tasks or equations, that it needs to solve in a small amount of time. Such a situation may arise because it wants to map or sequence the genome of humans, for instance. To achieve this, it could create a community cloud that has various universities across the world as its members and each such member contributes an equal amount of computing resources. The elastic nature of cloud computing would ensure that a constant number of computing resources are available at any given time, since those computers that are unused at night in a certain part of the world would be made available to work on the problem. Such a cloud would therefore not be confined to a single data center but be defined by computing resources spanning geographical boundaries and numerous data centers. The advantages in this case are obvious: cheaper computing resources through sharing, reduced computation time, and more efficient use of investment in IT infrastructure. The disadvantages are technical and commercial: greater emphasis is placed on the network, so it will probably require frequent upgrading, as will the network devices. Also, a legal framework will be needed that delineates who owns the intellectual property as well as the data across the community cloud.

The university community cloud is one example of the use of IaaS and PaaS for solving computation-intensive problems. A simpler example is when you want to render video images on the fly. Such an application would not call for a community cloud spanning geographies but would still call for a computing-intensive IaaS service to be provided. In such a scenario, an IaaS or PaaS cloud service would be ideal because you would want a high level of computing resources available only while the rendering is being performed. This means that you would only pay for the cloud service when needed during the rendering process; you would not need to invest capital upfront in buying computing resources that you may need only once in a while. Also, since the nature of image rendering is that you cannot assess and predict the amount of computing required, it makes sense to leverage the elasticity of a cloud platform. The major disadvantage will be for you to ensure that your Internet connection to the cloud service provider has the necessary bandwidth to meet your image rendering needs.

Another simple example of such a cloud computing use case is when you would want your applications to be hosted in the cloud so that your end-user device, such as a laptop or smart phone, provides you with a view of that single application. This use case would require your end-user device to be either a thin client device[1] or a zero-client device.[2] Such devices can be useless if stolen, and additionally are easy and cheap to replace when compared to desktops or laptops. Thus, large organizations can provide their employees with such "dumb" devices—terminals—that provide a view to cloud-hosted applications. This use case opens up a new business model opportunity for cloud and application service providers. They could give away the zero clients for free but ensure that the devices only connect to their cloud or to their application, for which a usage fee would be charged. This is akin to giving away razors for free while charging for the blades.

Web Hosting

Some of the characteristics of website hosting are (1) you have very little sense of the traffic; (2) the traffic can vary by time of day, week, or month; and (3) there can be bursts of traffic when a marketing campaign or a product launch occurs. These characteristics are in addition to the general requirement for infrastructure to scale as the business expands. The IaaS/PaaS cloud computing model is ideally suited to address these needs of web hosting because of its elasticity and usage-based pricing model.

Storage

The storage normally provided by IaaS or PaaS providers has built in redundancy. This means that if the individual disks that stored your data were to fail, you would still not lose your data since redundant disks would have the data. This type of storage comprises of redundant arrays of inexpensive disks (RAID) that are configured so that data are divided and replicated among the drives. In addition the disks are monitored so that should any disk fail, then it is replaced with another without any data loss. For a nontechnical person, and for small businesses, to install such a system locally is not generally possible because of the technical competence, monitoring, and configuration expertise involved. IaaS based cloud storage solutions are ideal since they are readily available, have usage-based price models, can be accessed from anywhere in the world, and can be accessed using any device. The data that you store can be media files (image, audio, video files, etc.), information relevant to you (your passwords, financial information, or asset information), correspondence (emails or letters), and general files (pdf files, spreadsheets, etc.) — indeed files that you need as a matter of course. Most commercial offerings for storage are Apple's iCloud, Dropbox, Google Drive, and Amazon S3.

Backup and Recovery
While writing this book, I had a mishap. In trying to upgrade my system disk, I changed the settings that inadvertently made the data disks unusable. The system disk had Windows 7 on it and the data disks had been configured as RAID 1 storage (one disk mirrored the other disk so that if a single disk were to fail, I would still have data on the other). My manuscript was stored on the data disks. Because I had fresh backups on my backup server, I went

ahead and reconfigured my data disks and formatted them. I then tried to copy the files from the backup server to the data disks. That is when I ran into a major problem. The software that I used to restore the files copied only some of the files and deleted all the files from the backup server! I now had no manuscript! Although I was able to recover a few files (each chapter was on an individual file), most of my work was lost. If I had used a cloud service provider as a backup, then I would not have had such a problem. Additionally, because my backup server and my workstation are at the same location, there was then still the risk of losing my files had a different type of disaster, such as a fire, occurred. The cloud service based backup would have a backup location that different from that of my own local workstation and backup server. The disadvantages of the cloud based backup are (1) risk of a security breach at the cloud service provider whereby a third-party can obtain your data, and (2) employees of the cloud service provider having access to your data. One way to overcome these disadvantages is to use a strong encryption mechanism and backup the encrypted files.

From a different perspective, let us suppose that you use a cloud service provider for data storage. It would make sense to appoint a different cloud service provider for backing up some or all of that data. There are two main reasons for using a different cloud service provider for backups: (1) you have a second location for your backups, and (2) you will retain access to your data if one provider had an outage or went out of business. A form of integration, or a simple application to backup and restore, would be needed between the two cloud service providers to ensure unrestricted data flow. One way to achieve this would be to synchronize the data between the two repositories using software such as freefilesync, rsync, or bit-torrent sync. Some of the commercial offerings available currently for backup include CrashPlan, Backblaze, Spideroak, Carbonite, Bitcasa, and Amazon Glacier. The latter is much more of an archival solution but can be used for incremental backup snapshots that you create once a month and plan to access only infrequently. The appendix at the end of this book provides a discussion of backup schemes.

Figure 22 shows the principal use cases for platform as a service. Some of these use cases are discussed below.

Database Services

A database is a collection of persistent data organized in such a way as to enable fast location and query of the data. The persistence of the data can be over the time for which an application runs or it can extend over much longer periods spanning multiple application instances and lifetimes. Typically, the characteristics of a database are (1) compactness, (2) speed of data retrieval and updates, and (3) currency, which ensures that the data remain relevant and up-to-date for your purposes. But you could think of a

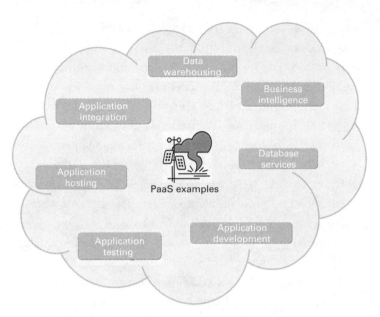

Figure 22   Use cases for platform as a service

database as simply an electronic filing system that has an index, records, and an organization to arrange the records for easy access. Because the database forms part of the integration and communication layer between applications, and thus enables multiple applications to share and reuse the same data, it is called middleware.

Underpinning a database is a storage system that physically stores the data for the database. So, besides the IaaS storage service discussed earlier, you could have a database system hosted on a PaaS service. This "database as a service" then ensures that you have a cloud cell that acts as a database system. Such a database service would need to be accessible easily and quickly for the applications that need to use it. So ideally you would want the database service to be in the same cloud as the applications that access it. This minimizes transaction times and provides optimum performance. The advantage of such a configuration is that you would have most of the IT stack in the cloud: the application, its database, and its physical storage. If the application were a web-based application, then you would access it remotely using a web browser, and if it were a "thick-client" application,[3] then you would use application virtualization (as explained in chapter 1) in order to access it, which can be a means to realize a thin-client or zero-client computing model.

Another advantage of having a cloud database service has to do with databases' usefulness to the extent that, for a variety of applications, they can be viewed as commodity items. As such, you could configure a database service as a cloud cell that acts as an appliance. This means that every time you needed to have a database, you would not need to specify, install, and configure one; you would instead just call up the database cloud cell within your cloud environment and link it to your application. That way, you would save time, effort, and expense by using the database-as-a-service cell. One of the major impediments of devising and using database cloud cells is commercial. Most companies do not have licensing policies that are amenable to such a cloud computing pattern or paradigm. One way of overcoming this difficulty is to use a free, open source, database such as PostgreSQL or MySQL.

Yet another advantage of a database cloud service is that applications hosted on disparate platforms that use different technologies can very easily access and query the records of a database system in a seamless manner. Accessibility of a database is further enhanced when using it as a cloud-based service as access is provided to the information from anywhere in the world using disparate applications and platforms. This is because database systems are very mature, in IT terms, and have various technology agnostic protocols, such as JDBC (Java Database Connectivity) and ODBC (Open Database Connectivity), for connectivity. In addition to these, most databases use a well-defined language called SQL (Structured Query Language) for querying, updating, and modifying database records. As a result, applications at different locations can become highly integrated with the use of a cloud-based database service.

Application Development
There are two main reasons why you may want to develop an application in the cloud using a PaaS service: (1) you

want to create an SaaS offering that you can use to go to market quickly, or (2) you want to go through the develop-build-test-deploy application life cycle quickly by concentrating on the application requirements without having to worry about the infrastructure stack. (After all, an application developer is not a data-center company and instead wants to focus on the application it provides.) In any case, there are a number of advantages to using PaaS for application development:

• Enables you to focus on creating the application, not peripheral things like the hardware.

• With the consumption-based price model you do not have to pay for the infrastructure up front.

• You can create applications that scale from one to upward of a million users without having to re-architect your application.

• Components such as storage and databases are available as standard, ready-made, off-the-shelf services for your application to use.

• You are provided with a standardized development environment that is familiar to most application developers. This can additionally include an application framework, code samples and development tools.

Although most cloud providers allow you to migrate your application, and tools exist to assist you, a major disadvantage is that a good application development environment locks you in to a particular vendor. The indirect costs associated with leaving, such as setting up your own environment elsewhere—obtaining the necessary talent, and the application integration work needed, for instance—can be too high for you to leave the cloud service provider. In order to mitigate this risk, you need to (1) assess the technology and application development framework provided by the PaaS service and (2) ensure that your application and data architecture allow for greater interoperability and flexibility.

Commonly used cloud platforms currently are Microsoft's Azure, Google's App Engine, and Amazon's Elastic Compute Cloud (EC2). To a large extent, these three offerings are not comparable directly because they offer different things, even though you could write the same set of applications on each platform. Azure provides you with the .Net framework. This is a software framework that includes a library of re-usable software that provides interoperability between various programming languages (e.g., Visual Basic, C, C++, and C#). This means that code written in any one supported language can reuse code written in the other languages. App Engine, however, provides you with a runtime environment for which you can write code in Python, Java, PHP, and Go. It allows you to develop and test your code using the App Engine runtime environment and optionally use Eclipse as an IDE.[4] These characteristics of the App Engine align it to a web application or one targeted to a mobile device. Amazon's EC2 is much more of an application hosting platform than an application development platform, and it is much more of an IaaS service than a PaaS one. However, it can be used for application development and testing, although you will need to set up your own application framework, tools, and development stack. Thereafter, you will need to maintain and upgrade it yourself. Also, the onus of making your application scalable is yours, since you get a high degree of freedom and control over your hardware. As a result, its main advantage is that you can migrate far more easily away from EC2 should you wish to do so in future.

Application Testing

Much of the discussion on application development applies to testing as well. Testing serves two purposes: it validates the user requirements are right for the application, and it verifies that the application meets those requirements. The main benefits of using cloud services for testing are:

• Test environment can double up as a demo environment.

• Flexible testing environment available without any capital costs.

•   Flexibility to ramp up or down as your testing needs change.

•   Ease of migration between multiple environments (demo, development, testing, etc.).

•   Standardized test tools, procedures, and test scripts if environment is shared with your client; this is especially useful for beta and user acceptance testing.

•   Agility to go to market as timescales for setting up test environments are reduced.

•   Software sizing and volumetric information gained from simulated users help to assess scalability and infrastructure needs.

You can use the cloud-based test environment to perform various tests. Alpha and beta tests, disaster recovery tests, functional tests, integration tests, load tests, operations tests, parallel running tests, performance tests, stress tests, security tests, system tests, unit tests, and user acceptance tests are the most common types of testing.

Application Integration
In order to integrate business processes and functions, you need to integrate the applications and the data used by those functions. Middleware provides the integration layer that enables you to do this. There are three types of

middleware: (1) message oriented, (2) data oriented, and (3) object oriented. Message-oriented middleware allows applications to send messages among themselves, essentially through the use of message queues. Data-oriented middleware allows the applications to share chunks of data and information among them, through the exigency of a database. Object-oriented middleware allows applications to share objects such as code—a common use is for an application to execute code in another application. We have dealt with data-oriented middleware in this chapter under the heading "Database Services," so we will consider message-oriented middleware in this section as a tool to integrate applications and, in a wider context, cloud-based services.

Message-oriented middleware relies on message queues in order to exchange messages among applications. A message queue is defined in memory as a buffer, a dataset in a database or a file set on a disk. Messages are sent to the queue by the sender application, and they accumulate until they are retrieved by receiver applications. The characteristic advantages of message-oriented middleware can be adduced by its delivery model, as follows.

Synchronicity   You can have synchronous or asynchronous messaging. The latter characteristic means that you can have applications that do not wait upon each other to exchange messages. Having synchronous messaging, also known as blocked messaging, ensures that one job is completed based on the processing or reception of a message before another job begins, since the sending application will wait until a message has been read before sending another message.

Decoupling Decoupling enables the communicating applications to be independent functionally and physically. They could reside on different infrastructure, use different technologies, and have different logic embedded in the code, thus providing a resilient solution.

Quality of Service (QoS) There are three different QoS levels: (1) assured or reliable, (2) guaranteed, and (3) transacted. Assured messages depend on a handshake mechanism whereby the receiving application tells the sending one that its message (or sequential block of messages) has been received. Guaranteed messaging delivers a message such that it is sent once, and once only, with the assurance that it will be delivered to the receiving application. Guaranteed messaging usually employs message persistence as a mechanism to ensure that delivery takes place even if the sender or receiver become unavailable during the time the message is sent and is in transit but has not yet been received. Transacted messages ensure that the message is part of a transaction, or end-to-end business function, such that the message is deemed to have been delivered only when the transaction as a whole is committed or completed.

Messaging Ordering and Filtering   You can send and retrieve messages between communicating applications in terms of their priority, group, or identity. By assigning a priority to messages, you can ensure that higher priority messages are retrieved first; otherwise, without an assigned priority, messages are normally retrieved from message queues on a first-come, first-served basis (in IT parlance, this is called FIFO—first in, first out). Alternatively, for sender application identification reasons or to correlate messages to certain tasks, you could assign identifiers to the messages. This enables you to process a stream of related messages only when all the messages related by a common identifier have been received. Another reason for identifiers is if you wanted to create a sequence of messages within groups. You could then identify a message within a group of messages on the basis of its identification. You could even have group identifiers to then identify message groups.

Message Type   You can have different types of messages on the basis of anonymity and linkage. With the former, you can have anonymous or nonanonymous messages that contain information relevant to the sending application. With the latter, you can have point-to-point messages between a sender and a receiver or receivers, or you can have broadcast messages that allow receivers interested in a particular topic to receive messages sent under that topic. Having the right message type and maintaining consistency allows you to deploy queues locally or in a distributed fashion between clients and servers in client-server architecture, thus providing you with the capability to create scalable applications and business functions.

Security   To ensure that only applications that you want to receive messages receive them, you can have access control to the queue such that applications that have the right credentials are authorized to retrieve messages from the queue. Also, you can have similar access controls in place for senders so that only authorized applications can send messages to a particular queue.

While considering application integration, it is important for you to define a message model or data model that will enable the applications to exchange data when using message or data-oriented middleware. The common data model will ensure that you can maintain the decoupling between applications without binding the data closely to the business logic embedded within the application. Some industries have standard data models such as fpML, SWIFT, and FIX in the finance industry.

Commercial offerings for application integration include IBM Websphere MQ, Tibco Rendezvous, RabbitMQ,

Beanstalkd, and Amazon SQS. Apart from the latter, none are cloud-based services. However, you can install them in your cloud to integrate your applications and business processes. Amazon SQS is a distributed queue system that enables web applications to send messages between the applications' components within Amazon's cloud service. You can integrate SQS with Amazon's CloudWatch, a service that monitors cloud resources and applications, to collect, view, and analyze usage metrics for your SQS queues.

SWOT Analysis

Figure 23 provides a SWOT analysis of the IaaS and PaaS cloud computing models from the point of view of the cloud user. Many of the weaknesses, especially around data security and integrity, can be addressed by employing various tactics. One such tactic is to employ encryption that encrypts your sensitive data stored in the cloud or used by your applications in the cloud. Another tactic is to use a hybrid cloud model whereby the IaaS/PaaS service is used as a compute node and your data are stored locally or with a different IaaS/PaaS provider. These options are not mutually exclusive, so you may combine them to meet enhanced security requirements. Both options, however, suffer from the drawback of an extra time lag that would be incurred when your applications encrypt and decrypt the

Strengths	Weaknesses
• No up-front investment in infrastructure • Pay for what you use and when you use it • Specify or use your own operating system • Install your own tools and applications • Scale easily to meet demand variations • Automatic backup of system • High availability from any location	• Security may be compromised • Cloud service provider has access to your data and applications • Low visibility of whether the CPU count or RAM is sufficient for the application and its users

Opportunities	Threats
• Ability to go to market quickly • Greater synergy with market ecosystem when using a community cloud • Capability to contain security threats with a hybrid cloud model • Small businesses or startups can obtain economies of scale for infrastructure	• Increased reliance on cloud service provider

Figure 23 SWOT analysis for infrastructure and platform as a service

data on the fly usually by invoking an encryption/decryption service.[5]

Understanding the load placed by the application and its users is a universal consideration that is not only confined to cloud computing. Applications need to be tested properly in terms of the size of RAM and number of CPU cores they will need in order to provide optimum user experience. Unfortunately, this hardly ever gets done, and the "application testing" use case for IaaS/PaaS cloud model can certainly help in this regard. In any case, the major advantage of cloud computing can in a sense become one of its weaknesses: it throws resources, via elasticity, in order to meet demand rather than provide you with the visibility of the relationship between computing resources used in

Table 4 Key takeaways: infrastructure as a service (IaaS)

Scope	Private, community, public, and hybrid clouds
Common uses	IT infrastructure services, such as storage, printing, computing, networking, and hosting
Examples	• File synchronization (Dropbox) • Printing (Google Print) • Hosting (Amazon EC2, HP Cloud, and Rackspace) • Storage (Amazon Cloud Drive and JustCloud) • Backup (ZipCloud and Carbonite)
Questions to ask	• Is there a minimum term applicable contractually? • Is there any element of CapEx? • Are there any penalties that apply to the service provider if SLAs are not met? • How transparent are the SLAs? What metrics will be monitored and reported? • How often are the reports updated? • Are there any business continuity or disaster recovery measures in place? • What are the end-to-end transaction times? Do these degrade during peak usage?
Common price models	Usually based on storage consumed, computing resources used, or network traffic—or a combination of these. Generally, OpEx is used for public clouds. There can be a CapEx element for private, community, and hybrid clouds.

Table 5 Key takeaways: platform as a service (PaaS)

Scope	**Private, community, public, and hybrid clouds**
Common uses	Application support services, such as database hosting, application hosting, application development, and testing
Examples	• Testing (user-acceptance tests, alpha tests, beta tests, integration tests, unit tests, functional and nonfunctional tests) • Integration (file translation, data transformation to/from XML data models) • Development (C, C++, Net, Java based application development) • Database services (business intelligence and data-warehousing) • Web hosting using LAMP (Linux-Apache-MySQL-PHP/Perl) stack or Microsoft.Net IAAS • Application hosting
Questions to ask	Similar to IaaS: • Is there a minimum term applicable contractually? • Is there any element of CapEx? • Are there any penalties that apply to the service provider if SLAs are not met? • How transparent are the SLAs? • What metrics will be monitored and reported? • For testing purposes, is data scrubbing required? • Does any data need to be archived?
Common price models	Usually OpEx; minimum terms may apply contractually for the service to be consumed

proportion to the demand. This is really a monitoring and reporting feature that many cloud service providers should make available to you routinely.

The threat of being reliant on a cloud service provider only exists when the service you outsource to the cloud is critical to your business. Then you will need to create business continuity plans that will allow you to continue business operations in a seamless fashion in the event that you lose access to the cloud service.

USE CASE PATTERN #2: SAAS

We build on IaaS and PaaS cloud services from the previous chapter by similarly identifying a common theme for SaaS cloud computing in terms of use cases. We consider various use cases for SaaS and follow up with a SWOT analysis of the SaaS cloud computing model from your—the user's—perspective. We conclude with a key takeaway section that considers some of the questions you would need to ask when deliberating over a SaaS offering from a cloud service provider.

Use Cases for SaaS

Software comprises those applications that are installed on a computer and provide a known function to you, the user of the computer. For the purposes of cloud computing, any software that runs in the background for supporting integration and monitoring purposes is termed middleware, and not "software." A distinct function that you may want your computer to provide for you can be, for example, office productivity (word processing, presentation, emails, analysis functions using spreadsheets, etc.), tracking assets within your home or organization, budgeting and financial planning, and billing and invoicing to clients. These are some of the use cases for software as a service, as figure 24 shows.

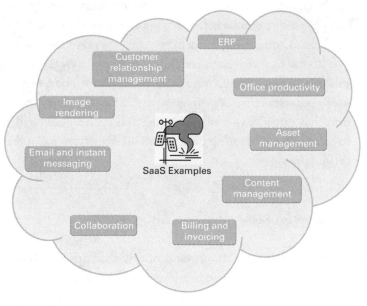

Figure 24   Use cases for software as a service

To get a taste of the pros and cons of using software as a service, let us consider some of the use cases of figure 24.

Customer Relationship Management

Customer relationship management (CRM) helps you to manage your company's interactions with current and prospective customers. In a sense, a CRM application is contact management that allows you to describe the client and create a follow up strategy. Additionally, it provides you with reporting and dashboards to assess various customer growth and attrition metrics. Because it is relatively easy to write CRM code for the cloud and also because CRM can be a standalone piece of software that many businesses have a need for, regardless of their business model, most CRM offerings are SaaS offerings. Commonly available CRM SaaS offerings are Microsoft Dynamics and Salesforce CRM.

The major advantages of using an SaaS-based CRM solution is to be able to access customer records from anywhere in the world, be able to track and assess your sales team's performance in a standardized and objective manner, and have an instant idea of your revenue growth profile. Disadvantages are (1) that you rely on the SaaS provider, and (2) that your customer related data may not be secure. The latter is a risk that arises from the possibility of the SaaS vendor being attacked by hackers or its employees having access to your data. However minimal this risk might be, it is a risk that you will need to accept

The major advantages of using an SaaS-based CRM solution is to be able to access customer records from anywhere in the world, be able to track and assess your sales team's performance in a standardized and objective manner, and have an instant idea of your revenue growth profile.

as a cost to your business. The former refers to your SaaS vendor having an outage or going out of business. You can mitigate this risk somewhat by ensuring that you backup your CRM data regularly with a different cloud provider.

Billing and Invoicing

In the same way as you have IT infrastructure, you have business infrastructure that performs central functions such as human resource management, asset tracking, billing, invoicing, and auditing. These functions are part of your business operations but are not part of your business model. You could effectively outsource these by using an SaaS or a BPaaS service instead. Billing and invoicing is an example use case in this stable.

When your customers place an order, the automated acknowledgment, billing, invoicing, and settlement can be outsourced to a third party. The third party that performs all those tasks as a sequence of events essentially provides a business function. And if that business function is automated and hosted in the cloud, then it is a business process as a service as in the case of PayPal's acquirer[1] service. If, however, you installed your billing and invoicing application on a PaaS platform and your employees then used it as part of their work, then it would be a private SaaS offering. You could even create your own process that integrates your own SaaS based invoicing with PayPal to get an end-to-end billing and settlement service.

The main advantage of having such a SaaS-based capability is to create efficiencies in your cash flow by automating mundane tasks so that you and your employees concentrate on your main business.

Collaboration, Instant Messaging, and Email

Many people use Outlook for emailing, Lync for instant messaging, and tools such as Lync and Sharepoint for collaboration. From a nonspecialist's viewpoint, these tools and activities can be categorized as group communication activities. Notice that mostly they are all tools provided by Microsoft for use on a Windows desktop. Likewise, Apple provides comparable tools for the Apple desktop. Of course there are third-party, off-the-shelf, tools available from independent vendors, but these tend not to have the same number of users. With cloud computing, the locus is changing from the operating system, at the device level, to a more distributed landscape. This levels the field. Indeed, relatively new entrants to this field, such as Google, now provide similar tools for free via the cloud as a delivery model. Further notice that all these tools are essentially commodity, everyday use, type of "business infrastructure" tools that your business needs in order to function on a routine basis.

There is yet another disruptor of communication. Often the end-user devices are not specified by the IT department, and instead there is a drive to encourage you to bring your own device (BYOD) to work. The combination of cloud computing, thin or zero clients, and BYOD effectively means that the traditional form of group communication is undergoing a systemic shift to the cloud and to a more distributed computing model. And increasingly the trend is to use the cloud-based tools in preference to the desktop ones. However, you need to be conscious of the reasons to migrate to the cloud, away from the desktop, when adopting these tools because they are vital to your business. Below are four core principles that you will need to adhere to when considering a cloud model.

• **Security: Trust Your Employees**   Rather than restrict your employees by specifying technologies they should use in order to enforce security, you trust them to be honest and responsible. Of course, you could stipulate that they store your data in an encrypted or sandboxed environment on their own device in the case of BYOD. That way, any malware they pick up on their personal devices will not affect your business.

• **Dependency or Lock-In: Have an Alternative, Just in Case**   If possible, store your documents on an IaaS storage platform provided by a third party instead of the productivity tools vendor. Make sure that you backup your documents to a different location and with a different vendor so that you are not entirely dependent on any one vendor. The best practice is to store your documents in an open file format, such as RTF or ODF, so that other applications will be able to access them.

• **Cost: Consider the Total Cost of Ownership** Just considering the application license costs is not enough. You need to consider costs related to application packaging, distribution, and maintenance as well. Maintenance relates to ensuring that the current versions and service packs for the applications are installed. As such, you will most likely find the cloud based solution to be more cost efficient.

• **Focus: Concentrate on Your Business Model** If your business is not in IT and you do not need to have a large IT department as an overhead, then it makes sense for you to use SaaS as a means to concentrate on your core business values and drivers.

The advantages of using cloud-based SaaS offerings are obvious: cost of ownership is low and you get the freedom to concentrate on your core business offerings without being distracted by IT infrastructure or business infrastructure related matters. But you could go one step further. Instead of having a mail server for emails that use your business's domain, you could just use commercial mail offerings (e.g., Google mail or Yahoo mail) for your emails. Thus your company email address would then be, for instance, <employee name>.<company name>@[yahoo, gmail, or whatever].com. And if you definitely did want to have a business domain, then you could point your domain to route mails to the commercial mail offerings. (People would then email you at yourbiz.com, your domain name, but you would retrieve those emails at Google or Yahoo.) This would then be in the true spirit of BYOD and cloud computing.

Office Productivity
As the locus shifts from the desktop to the cloud, the same considerations apply for office productivity tools as they do for group communications. Office productivity tools encompass word processing, presentation, and spreadsheet software. These applications have been installed in the cloud by various companies, such as Microsoft and Google, and are available to you as SaaS offerings. Microsoft provides Office 365 for you to use from the cloud, and Google provides Google Docs, Sheets, and Slides that let you create online documents, work on them in real time with other people, and store them in your cloud storage online. As most of the computing power is expended in the cloud, it stands to reason that you need less powerful client devices to work with online documents. As such, intrinsically related to SaaS are thin- and zero-client devices. Chrome Books (thin-client laptops) and Chrome Boxes (thin-client desktops) are examples of such devices.

Zero-client devices, such as the HP 410t, additionally allow you to use application virtualization should you need to use a single device to access your fat-client applications that you host in your private cloud as well as access office productivity applications that are hosted by third parties in a public cloud.

Image Rendering

Recall that we considered image rendering as a possible use case for IaaS in the preceding chapter. If you were to install the image rendering software on the IaaS platform and make it available as a cloud service, then it effectively becomes SaaS because the users of the software then just use it in the cloud. This is an example of building on IaaS by installing software that is available to others in a multi-tenant environment to create an SaaS offering. You can go up the abstraction stack from IaaS to PaaS to SaaS to INaaS to BPaaS by adding greater value at each stage—think of it as an abstraction-value ladder.

SWOT Analysis

Figure 25 shows a SWOT analysis of the SaaS cloud computing abstraction from the point of view of the cloud user.

Strengths	Weaknesses
• No up-front infrastructure costs for hosting utility applications • No up-front license, packaging, or maintenance costs for utility applications that are available as SaaS • Ability to increase cash flow efficiencies by automating mundane tasks • Focus on your core business values and drivers, and not be distracted by IT	• Dependency on a SaaS provider's data format. This can be addressed by exporting files in open formats and using a different vendor for backups • Interoperability between one SaaS provider and another due to their different applications, billing cycles, or SLAs

Opportunities	Threats
• Use Bring-Your-Own-Device (BYOD) in conjunction with SaaS • Use thin or zero clients with both public SaaS applications and your own fat-client applications hosted in a private cloud • Ability to move up the Abstraction-Value ladder to increase productivity and efficiency via automation	• Security can be compromised as a result of infiltration of the SaaS vendor or employees of the vendor having access to your data. This can be mitigated somewhat by ensuring that personally identifiable data is not stored in the cloud as much as possible when using SaaS

Figure 25 SWOT analysis for software as a service

Table 6   Key takeaway: software as a service (SaaS)

Scope	Private, community, public, and hybrid clouds
Common uses	Commodity applications; applications that are used commonly by most people or businesses
Examples	<ul><li>Email services</li><li>Office productivity suite (Google Docs or Microsoft Office 365)</li><li>Customer relationship management (salesforce)</li><li>Image rendering (HP Cloud solutions for media)</li><li>Content Management (Box, SpringCM, and Microsoft)</li></ul>
Questions to ask	Similar questions to IaaS and PaaS:<ul><li>Is there a minimum term applicable contractually?</li><li>Is there any element of CapEx?</li><li>Are there any penalties that apply to the service provider if SLAs are not met?</li><li>How transparent are the SLAs? What metrics will be monitored and reported?</li><li>How often are the reports updated?</li><li>Are there any business continuity or disaster recovery measures in place?</li><li>What are the end-to-end transaction times? Do these degrade during peak usage?</li></ul>
Common price models	Usually OpEx on the basis of volumetrics such as number of users, mailboxes, or storage consumed by email

USE CASE PATTERN #3: INAAS

In IT's domain of knowledge management, an important distinction is made regarding data, information, and knowledge. Data do not possess any context to your particular situation or need, information is contextual data, and knowledge is information with expertise or experience in its usability. So, for instance, you might have data regarding all the flights in the world but only the data that apply to your holiday schedule are relevant—that is information. Knowledge in this case would be the flight information that will get you to your destination with the least trouble to you (lost luggage, stopovers, flight delays, etc.).

There is a pitfall that you ought to be aware of. When data (or data storage) are delivered to you as a service, it is really PaaS, not INaaS because you are consuming the use of the infrastructure. And data storage or delivery has many forms: DropBox, Google Drive, or Apple's iCloud are examples of data storage. Flight, train, and bus timetables are largely data unless there is a supplementary

Data do not possess any context to your particular situation or need, information is contextual data, and knowledge is information with expertise or experience in its usability.

service (e.g., obtaining your location using GPS and then providing you with the appropriate bus or train times in real-time) that would make it an INaaS cloud service. One method you can use to distinguish between PaaS and INaaS is to think of raw data offerings as PaaS; when the data has some form of software or application that transforms it, then the data becomes information and its delivery becomes INaaS; when a business process acts on information to augment it with expertise, then that knowledge delivery becomes BPaaS. Thus data need to be augmented by software for it to become information; information needs to be augmented by a process for it to become knowledge.

When data (or its storage) is delivered to you as a cloud service, it is PaaS; when information is delivered, it is known as information as a service (INaaS); when knowledge is delivered, it is business process as a service (BPaaS).

We consider the use cases of INaaS in this chapter. We also perform a SWOT analysis for INaaS so that you may be aware of its strengths and weaknesses. This should provide you with sufficient background to assess whether a particular INaaS is suitable for you.

Use Cases for INaaS

The following characteristics define INaaS:

- It integrates and is composed of these cloud service models: IaaS, PaaS, and SaaS.

- It has a well-defined set of interfaces that allows it to integrate and communicate with other applications or software in your organization.

- It is flexible enough to be reconfigured to meet new or changes in business needs and drivers.

- It can be available in any of the deployment models, such as private, public, hybrid, or community.

- In common with other cloud services, it provides scalability through elasticity. Thus it should support varying numbers of users.

- It uses automation wherever possible. The service often incorporates data and augments it with logic embedded in software to create meaningful information.

- It uses consumption or utility-based price models.

The advantages of INaaS are (1) data that are meaningful to you, (2) increased productivity through instantaneous and current information, (3) standardization across business units and geographies, (4) increased agility from its currency and immediacy, and (5) cost or cash flow efficiency resulting from the pricing model.

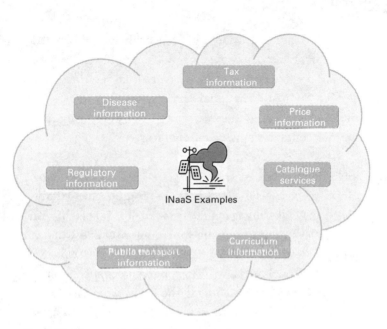

Figure 26   Use cases for information as a service

Figure 26 shows some of the principal use cases for information as a service. In particular, we discuss below INaaS cloud services related to: regulations, taxation, price, health and curricula.

Regulatory Information

A number of regulatory frameworks exist. Some are specific to an organization's country of incorporation; some are specific to the industry; and others, such as those related to money laundering, are worldwide. Information that pertains to these regulations as applicable to a particular organization can be delivered as an INaaS cloud service. For a multinational corporation, this service is especially useful in gathering information pertaining to the various countries in which it operates

Tax Information
Once a year—sometimes more frequently—taxation codes and rules change in most countries. If this information, relevant to your situation, were available wherever and whenever you needed it, then that would be an example of an INaaS use case. You would expect such a service to be in heavy demand during the times when people and businesses need to file their tax returns, so there is a peak in demand over a few weeks in a year. Thus the elasticity afforded by cloud computing makes it worthwhile for a tax information provider to commission an INaaS.

Price Information
Having the price of a product is having data related to the product; having the price of a product you want to purchase is akin to having information. Thus, if you are walking down a street and the weather becomes overcast, what if an application informed you that the nearest shops to your location that stocked umbrellas or raincoats had certain price offers? That would be having price information

as a service, since it would be meaningful data that applies to your situation.

Disease- and Health-Related Information

With the advent of a number of wearable devices, health monitoring is increasingly becoming a reality. Using that health monitoring data to provide you (or anyone you nominate such as your doctor or your family member) with an alert should a certain level be reached is an obvious progression. Incorporating predictive capabilities to that data turns it into meaningful information as it tells you the chances of a certain condition occurring on the basis of the trends that may be identified. In addition, what if certain medical websites (e.g., WebMD) could be trawled instantaneously so that you had relevant information related to the extrapolated trends in your health? It would allow you to be much more pro-active and, on an aggregate level, increase the well-being of the citizens.

Curriculum Information

The various courses you take at school have timetables related to the lectures, tests, laboratory sessions, and homework assignments. Having at hand information that relates to your specific course of study at school and relevant only to you solely would be akin to having a personal assistant. And this would be applicable for every student, regardless of the school or course they were attending. Such an information service is an example of an INaaS use case.

SWOT Analysis

Figure 27 provides a SWOT analysis of the INaaS cloud computing abstraction from your point of view as a cloud user.

Strengths	Weaknesses
• Instantaneous availability of the latest information related to your application or project • Filter out information that is not relevant to your application or project • Pay only for the information that you need	• Not all the information from a public INaaS provider would be relevant to you • Small likelihood of similar information being provided by a different vendor, which can mean that you are locked in with a single vendor • Legal and compliance issues need to aligned regularly between you and your cloud vendor, as these might change over time

Opportunities	Threats
• Create a mash of information from different providers to create an information set that is relevant to you • Opportunity to incorporate INaaS with SaaS from disparate cloud service providers to create your own BPaaS • Multiple uses of the same information throughout your organization or across a number of applications	• Dependence on a third-party to provide information that may be critical to your business's operation • Information protection and privacy would need to be considered as a breach can have devastating consequences

Figure 27 SWOT analysis for Information-As-A-Service

Table 7 Key takeaway: Information as a service (INaaS)

Scope	**Private, community, public, and hybrid clouds**
Common uses	Information services or data analyzed or refreshed to make it situation or location aware
Examples	• Price information (stocks and commodity prices at various exchanges) • Stock information of its key metrics (P/E ratio, yield, etc.) • Provision of service catalogs and the related SLAs and costs • Health information from monitoring patients or aggregated health metrics on organizations' performances • Real-time flight, train, or bus information Regulatory information • Information pertaining to tax rules, and the tax levels and rates
Questions to ask	• How current is the information? • How accurate is the information? • Is the information relevant (i.e. suited to your needs, situation or location)? • Are there privacy or data protection laws pertaining to the information? • Are there industry, national, or global regulations pertaining to the information? • Will the information need to be backed up? If so, how (which backup scheme—refer to the appendix at the end of the book) and with what service? • Will the information need to be archived? If so, for how long? How will the information be destroyed once its archival period ends? • What security measures are used to protect your information? In particular: (1) will the information be compromised when you receive it? (2) what measures do you need to follow in order to keep it secure? (3) who is allowed to use the information? and (4) is encryption required? • What metrics apply to assess the relevance, currency, and accuracy of the information?
Common price models	Usually OpEx on the basis of information consumed; yearly, quarterly, or monthly contractual terms may apply

USE CASE PATTERN #4: BPAAS

BPaaS delivers a vertical or horizontal business process using a workflow, cloud computing technologies, and price models in an automated or semi-automated manner. It is the highest abstraction level in cloud computing and so is based on, and uses, the other abstraction levels (IaaS, PaaS, SaaS, and INaaS) in delivering the service. Vertical processes are processes that are part of the business model, and horizontal processes are processes that support the vertical ones as ancillary services.

Figure 28 shows examples of vertical and horizontal processes at a high-level for five different industry segments. Underlying each process, whether vertical or horizontal, is a distinct workflow. Let us illustrate the concept by employing the example of a café. Suppose that you are in a café, you place an order for latte, pay your bill, find a place to sit while the coffee is made, and then get served at your table. That is a workflow. However, it can be divided

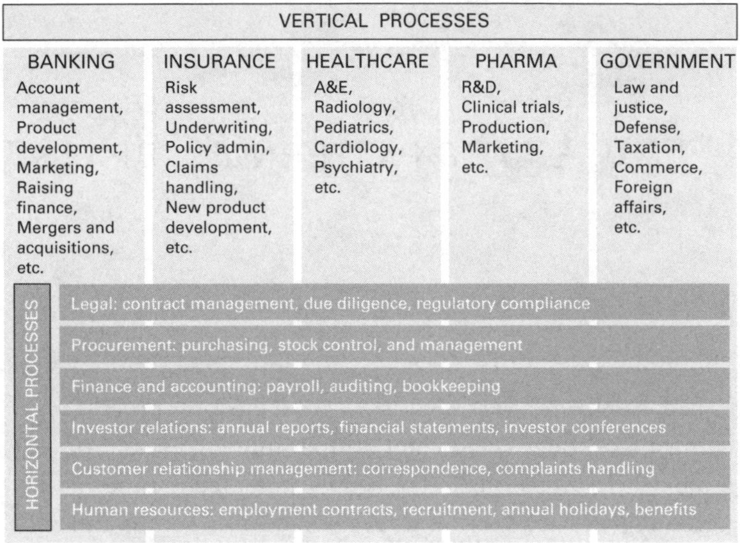

VERTICAL PROCESSES				
BANKING	**INSURANCE**	**HEALTHCARE**	**PHARMA**	**GOVERNMENT**
Account management, Product development, Marketing, Raising finance, Mergers and acquisitions, etc.	Risk assessment, Underwriting, Policy admin, Claims handling, New product development, etc.	A&E, Radiology, Pediatrics, Cardiology, Psychiatry, etc.	R&D, Clinical trials, Production, Marketing, etc.	Law and justice, Defense, Taxation, Commerce, Foreign affairs, etc.

HORIZONTAL PROCESSES

Legal: contract management, due diligence, regulatory compliance

Procurement: purchasing, stock control, and management

Finance and accounting: payroll, auditing, bookkeeping

Investor relations: annual reports, financial statements, investor conferences

Customer relationship management: correspondence, complaints handling

Human resources: employment contracts, recruitment, annual holidays, benefits

Figure 28   Vertical and horizontal business processes

into further workflows. For example, when making your coffee, the staff member selects the beans, puts them into the machine, cleans the pipes, boils the water to the right temperature, adds milk, and transfers the coffee to a cup. Most of these processes in the workflow, apart from the coffee machine making the coffee, are manual. (Of course, they could have been automated by the use of robotics or other technologies.) Regardless, whether automated or not, your café employed a number of business processes in serving you the coffee to your requirements. Some of these processes are outsourced to others. For instance, the staff member making your coffee "outsourced" the serving of the coffee to an attendant who brought it to you at your table; they also "outsourced" the ordering of more coffee beans and their stock control to some other person. Similarly there are many instances where entire business processes, or their constituent processes, can be outsourced to the cloud. In this chapter we will mostly consider horizontal processes as they are common to most business.

Use Cases for BPaaS

The following characteristics define BPaaS:

•   It integrates and is composed of the other cloud service models: IaaS, PaaS, SaaS, and INaaS.

•   It has a well-defined set of interfaces that allows it to integrate and communicate with other business processes in your organization.

•   It is flexible enough to be reconfigured to meet new or changes in business needs and drivers.

•   It can be available in any of the deployment models, such as private, public, hybrid, or community.

- In common with other cloud services, it provides scalability through elasticity. Thus it supports varying numbers of users of the business process.

- It uses automation wherever possible. The service can, however, be made up of workflows that are automated or manual.

- It uses consumption or utility-based price models.

The advantages of a BPaaS offering are (1) consistency and repeatability so that your Key Performance Indicator (KPI) metrics are met, (2) increased productivity through workflow automation, (3) standardization across business units, (4) increased agility through optimization, and (5) cost or cash flow efficiency resulting from the pricing model.

Figure 29 shows the principal use cases for business process as a service. We consider some of these below. In particular, we discuss (1) taxation and tax planning to demonstrate how BPaaS builds on SaaS and INaaS, (2) payroll functions as an example of a horizontal business process, (3) training to assess the changing landscape in education, (4) testing services to show how innovation is required not only in technology but also in business through the adaptation of different business processes, and (5) health monitoring to illustrate the art of the possible, especially with personal clouds. Although still very much in its infancy, BPaaS is foundational in terms of innovation in cloud

Although still very much in its infancy, BPaaS is foundational in terms of innovation in cloud computing, especially in the domains of personal clouds, cloud of things, and hybrid clouds that marry these two.

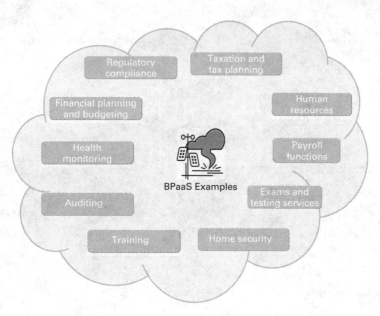

Figure 29   Use cases for business process as a service

computing, especially in the domains of personal clouds, cloud of things, and hybrid clouds that marry these two. We discuss such topics in more detail in chapter 11 on the future outlook of cloud computing.

Taxation and Tax Planning

Recall from the previous chapter the tax information use case for INaaS. For filling in tax returns and tax planning, you need to have the most recent tax information at hand.

Any business process that plans for tax therefore needs to receive information from an information service. Additionally, it needs to automate the information retrieval from the information service so that it always works with the most recent information available. For a BPaaS based tax planning system, it needs to use applications that help it to perform the various activities that form part of the process, such as data entry for the person, scenario-based projections, tax computations, and reporting. Those applications could be stand-alone or be hosted in the cloud, in which case they would be SaaS offerings. Such SaaS offerings can be from third parties available as cloud services in their own right. The business process then becomes a composite mash up of the various applications and the information that is orchestrated as a workflow to fulfill a purpose or business function. Of course, there can be human (or manual) interaction within the workflow, especially in assessing the suitability of various scenarios for the purposes of projecting future tax outlays. You can consider such a type of BPaaS offering as a cloud of clouds, where the BPaaS cloud service uses encapsulation principles that we discussed in chapter 2.

In summary, the common pattern with the taxation and tax planning use case is (1) encapsulation to create a composite BPaaS offering, and (2) the use of INaaS and SaaS as building blocks to deliver BPaaS. These paradigms are not mutually exclusive.

Payroll Functions

Payroll functions encompass the payment of salaries to employees, processing and mailing their pay slips, and sending tax to the government that has been deducted from the employees' pay. Most businesses that employ staff require such a business process regardless of the type of business they conduct. Hence, this business process is essentially a horizontal process, much like taxation and tax planning we discussed earlier.

Besides performing the activities within the payroll business process, there needs to be some interfacing with other processes. For example, when an employee takes unpaid leave, you need to ensure that the information from human resources is fed to the payroll process so that appropriate adjustments may be made to the pay. Also, if the employee is paid for working overtime, you need to have an interface with line management that ensures that those records are faithfully captured. Similarly, if an employee were to leave the company, then you want the business process for leavers run by human resources to let the payroll process know of the employee's last day at work. All this should illustrate that most business processes are not stand-alone—they need to interact with other processes in the business. When commissioning a BPaaS offering for such a business process, you should therefore establish the various interfaces needed to interact with other processes. These interfaces can be defined in terms of the data that need to be shared and the events that need to trigger the sharing of the data. Thus you require two forms of interfacing: control and information.

The advantages of using BPaaS for horizontal business processes such as payroll functions are (1) cost efficiency, especially for small and medium sized businesses, derived from efficiencies of scale; (2) consumption-based price model dependent on the number of records processed; and (3) standardized service delivery that performs to set KPI metrics. However, cloud-based business process offerings are currently quite few even though their SaaS components and manual counterparts do exist.

Training

BPaaS is inherently connected to Business Process Management (BPM) because it encapsulates business processes that have been defined by BPM. BPM is a set of methods, tools, and technologies used to design, enact, analyze, optimize, and control business processes. It has evolved and grown to include a number of techniques and technologies over time, as figure 30 illustrates. The main impetus for business process improvement came from manufacturing organizations becoming more process centric. This drive spawned techniques such as Just-In-Time and Six Sigma, which have been instrumental in making processes and businesses much more efficient. The delivery of training, not having been process centric, has largely escaped such a drive and has not adopted any BPM techniques as a result. The evolution of BPM has followed the trajectory from product centricity to process centricity, and the next phase in the cycle is to become customer centric. In other words, deliver what the customer wants, when they want it, in an efficient and scalable manner at the lowest cost base using the most optimized and efficient means. When training is delivered using BPaaS using the customer centric paradigm, it encapsulates the optimization and efficiency that the body of BPM knowledge can bring to bear. This is a powerful force for change as far as training is concerned.

Traditionally the delivery of training has not been scalable either. For instance, anyone wanting to receive formal training has had to go to a bricks-and-mortar college to learn from professors and in an environment where

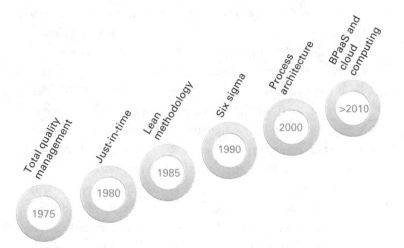

Figure 30 Evolution of business process management techniques and technologies

a group of people gather to receive the training together. This means that the training delivered has been restricted to those few that can be physically present at the institution depending, of course, on the capacity of the institution itself. Despite the existence of correspondence courses, scalability in terms of education and training has been lacking. However, various training sites such as Coursera and EdX have recently come to the forefront as deliverers of online training and educational courses. Video-sharing sites such as YouTube have also fulfilled a role in disseminating informal training. These are all scalable and have a compelling delivery model. Although none of them, however, use the BPaaS model, they do approach it; the next stage in their development could very easily be to offer training using the BPaaS service model. This could be done by the incorporation of the latest identification and authentication technologies when delivering training and testing using an integrated approach, from enrolment to certification.

Examinations and Testing Services
As goes training, so goes testing. The two are fundamentally related. Technology exists to establish whether the right person is taking a test and, further, is authorized to take it. Test questions can be chosen at random from a large bank of questions to ensure that the tests remain fair for everyone. Indeed test centers have sprung up to leverage this principle. However, why not take the tests in your own home? Why not take them as part of the learning experience rather

than after the course is over? With the use of web-cams and automated identification methods using voice biometrics, the technology certainly exists to provide a BPaaS based testing offering that is intrinsically integrated with training delivery. The education industry, however, needs to adapt and change their business processes. This then is a case of the technology innovation being far more advanced than business innovation. And the latter needs to happen in order to reap the benefits of the former.

In general, you will have noticed a trend emerge. Horizontal business processes are far more likely to be offered as BPaaS compared to vertical business processes. The reason is clear: vertical processes are part of the business and enmeshed with the business model; entrenched interests of the business stakeholders therefore create an atmosphere that is resistant to change for taking vertical processes to the cloud.

Health Monitoring
In healthcare, there is a drive to empower the patient or the individual to take charge of their health. Of course, this is very much dependent on changing attitudes, through education, of all the clinical stakeholders as well as the patient. Technology, however, can play a part in effecting such a change. Consider the following scenario: every individual has their own personal cloud—this is really a private cloud—which they use to store their health information, assess it so that an alert could be raised automatically in

case their health deteriorated, and have the option to send vital information to their doctor by email or instant messaging. This use case would also be helpful to clinicians that monitor bedridden or immobile patients in their homes. The personal cloud could even be augmented by interfaces to various wearable devices that monitor various parameters such as heart rate, weight, blood sugar level, and temperature. This would automate the monitoring, gathering of data, analysis, and alerting so that it would be akin to having a full-time nurse at your disposal.

Optionally, if individuals allowed certain anonymized data to be collated so that it could be aggregated, then you could create a general picture of the various morbidities or conditions affecting people on the basis of factors such as their age, sex, and geographic location. This could provide administrators or clinicians useful information in terms of demographics and their relation to morbidities in an objective manner. Further, you could use predictive analytics to assess the spread of various morbidities across regions and communities so that healthcare expertise can be better targeted. This would make the delivery of healthcare much more efficient, in the true spirit of BPM.

The main factor that the health monitoring use case of BPaaS provides is that conglomeration of various processes and techniques, some in the cloud and others outside, interact to create an automated workflow as part of the process. This gives you a cloud of people, analogous to the cloud of things.

SWOT Analysis

Figure 31 provides a SWOT analysis of the BPaaS cloud computing abstraction from the point of view of the cloud user.

Strengths	Weaknesses
• Flexibility allows for service to be reconfigured to meet changing needs • Available in any deployment model, such as private, public, hybrid, or community • Provides scalability to support varying numbers of users and load factors • Uses automation where possible to provide an efficient and optimized business process • Uses consumption or utility price model	• Need to clearly identify and implement interfaces with other business processes

Opportunities	Threats
• Cloud of clouds: use composition principles to create a mash-up of services that are orchestrated by a workflow to create BPaaS • Personal clouds: innovative use of private clouds to create personalized services	• Requires stakeholder buy-in since automation and optimization can result in a leaner workforce or changes in work practices

Figure 31   SWOT analysis of business process as a service

Table 8 Key takeaway: Business process as a service (BPaaS)

Scope	**Private, community, public, and hybrid clouds**
Common uses	Replaces a business process or a business function
Examples	• Human resource services • Testing/examination services • Training services • Health monitoring • Health pre-screening • Payroll functions • Regulatory compliance • Tax computation • Auditing • Ticketing and billing, etc.
Questions to ask	• Is there is an agreed checklist that is aligned to the business process or function being provided? • What processes at your company interact with the BPaaS cloud service? Do these need to be integrated and do they need to share any data? Are the interfaces defined clearly? • Are there any penalties applicable to the BPaaS provider if SLAs are not met? • What are the end-to-end transaction times for the service? How are these measured, reported and included in the SLAs?
Common price models	Usually OpEx on the basis of volumetric factors but can be fixed charge OpEx

TRANSITIONING TO THE CLOUD

Suppose you have decided that you want to use cloud computing. What next? How will you use the cloud services? How will those services interoperate with some other cloud services from a different vendor? We consider these key aspects of using a cloud service in this chapter. Additionally, you will need to assess the cloud service vendor in terms of your SLAs so that you may select the right cloud service provider as well as the right cloud service for you. If you were to look up SLAs and metrics on the Internet or the numerous books that have been written on cloud computing, you will frequently come across a discussion of SLA metrics such as network capacity (bandwidth, latency, or throughput), storage device capacity, server capacity (number of CPUs, CPU clock frequency, and RAM), instance starting time (time required to initialize a new instance of a virtual machine), horizontal storage scalability (defined as the permissible storage capacity changes in response to increased workloads), horizontal server scalability (server capacity changes in response to increased workloads expressed as number of virtual servers in a cloud's resource pool), and the list goes on to perhaps hundreds of such items! These SLAs are good if you need to create and operate your own cloud. But why should you, as a buyer and user of cloud services, need to worry about them? After all, cloud computing is supposed to provide a layer of abstraction that should minimize your technology headache, not increase it. We will therefore not follow the well-trodden route that most books on cloud computing take. We will instead examine SLAs and metrics that are relevant to you as a user of cloud services and, additionally, provide a checklist that you can adapt to assess cloud services. After discussing these requirements, we will examine the critical success factors for a typical cloud usage model. And, finally, we will discuss how you can assess your own maturity as a cloud service user by considering a cloud maturity model from a user's perspective. This way you can assess your cloud adoption with best-practices as well as track progress over time as you use cloud computing.

University Computing Model

The university computing model, also known as the Bring-Your-Own-Device (BYOD) model, is where you have complete diversity in the device you use in order to consume IT or cloud services. Recall, from chapter 3, that it got its name because students, unlike employees at a workplace, bring their own devices to school, and universities' IT departments have had to cater to a large variety of devices. Conversely, with most businesses, there is generally some form of homogeneity in the devices used as the IT department specifies which company devices can be used.

When you incorporate cloud computing to BYOD, a paradigm shift occurs in the delivery and consumption of IT services. As figure 32 shows, a number of parameters are affected when transitioning to BYOD. And this has repercussions with a number of disciplines in the organization: from finance to company policy.

Figure 32 shows how, for a given parameter, you would need to use a different approach with BYOD. Take data loss. With a company-specified device, you would have regular backups performed as specified by the central IT department; with BYOD, the data backup should be built in to your cloud-based storage. And the cloud-based storage itself ensures that you can access that data not only from any device but from anywhere in the world. Thus the flexibility and freedom afforded to a user increases markedly. Below we consider the different cloud usage models that are applicable to a computing environment.

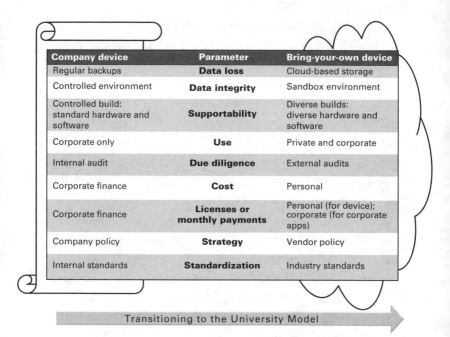

Company device	Parameter	Bring-your-own device
Regular backups	**Data loss**	Cloud-based storage
Controlled environment	**Data integrity**	Sandbox environment
Controlled build: standard hardware and software	**Supportability**	Diverse builds: diverse hardware and software
Corporate only	**Use**	Private and corporate
Internal audit	**Due diligence**	External audits
Corporate finance	**Cost**	Personal
Corporate finance	**Licenses or monthly payments**	Personal (for device); corporate (for corporate apps)
Company policy	**Strategy**	Vendor policy
Internal standards	**Standardization**	Industry standards

Transitioning to the University Model ➔

Figure 32 Transitioning to the university computing model

Cloud Usage Models

When transitioning to the cloud, you need to create a strategy[1] that considers the current, as-is, IT landscape and the future, to-be landscape, in order to create a plan of action. Generally, the IT landscape can be classified by the manner those services are delivered to you. There are five distinct usage models for the delivery and use of IT services, especially related to cloud computing. These are classified by the coupling IT has with the business. Figure 33 shows the first-generation usage model of cloud computing. This first-order usage model is based on a single IT service provider model that essentially provides services to an organization's business units with a central IT department controlling the SLAs and contracts. The single provider can appoint a third party to provide a set of services to the business units; the third party then acts as a subcontractor to the single provider. The service providers can supply a mix of services ranging from cloud computing to traditional IT.

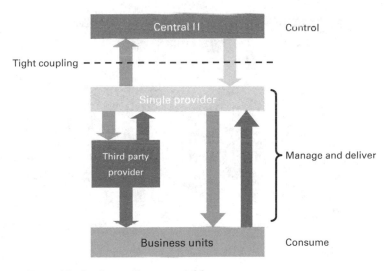

Figure 33   Single-provider usage model

The first-order usage model is the most commonly used model by organizations today. The main drawback of this model is the very tight coupling with the central IT department. This means that cloud services cannot respond in an agile manner to changing business requirements. A better model, however, is the one shown in figure 34 because it affords the flexibility to use multiple providers.

Thus, should a given provider's service not meet with changing business needs, then a different cloud service provider can be used for the needed services. The central IT department continues to act as a broker between the

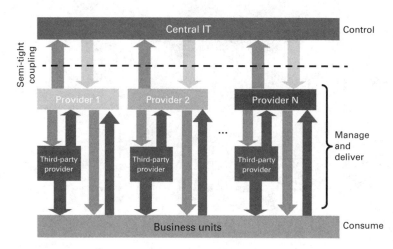

Figure 34 Multiple-provider usage model

business units and the cloud service providers. Additionally, it provides a key function—the integration of services. This integration function takes two forms: (1) to integrate the services among the various service providers, and (2) to integrate the business units with the providers. Although most organizations purport to use this model for IT services, whether or not related to cloud computing, they usually do not have such a model implemented because of the often insurmountable challenges that the central IT department faces in performing the integration function. One possibility is to appoint a service integrator (not a systems integrator!) to perform just such a function, as figure 35 shows.

The role of service integration is to ensure that a portfolio of IT products and services meets business needs in a consistent and efficient manner. The central IT department does not engage with the cloud service providers in such a model but works directly with the service integrator. Optionally, the service integrator could manage the contracts, reporting, and billing functions with the cloud service providers individually and then provide a consolidated report and bill to the central IT department. With this usage model, there is considerable flexibility for the business units to receive cloud services from three different parties: (1) the service integrator, (2) a third-party provider that the service integrator appoints, and (3) other service providers that the central IT department appoints. All these

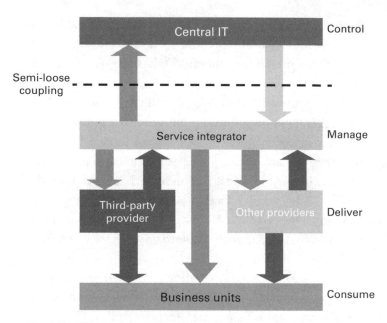

Figure 35 Third-order usage model with a service integrator

appointees provide services to the business units, with the central IT department still maintaining overall oversight of the cloud services on behalf of the business. But there still remains a problem over shadow IT,[2] and this problem is compounded greatly due to the convenience and flexibility afforded by cloud computing. One of the major issues that shadow IT opens up is an increased vulnerability to security breaches resulting from the nonstandard approach to IT taken by the business units. On the other hand, the reason why business units resort to shadow IT is because the usage models discussed so far lack the agility to meet business demands in a timely manner. A usage model that addresses these issues is therefore required; its main characteristic is to have loose coupling between the central IT department and the cloud service providers as figure 36 shows.

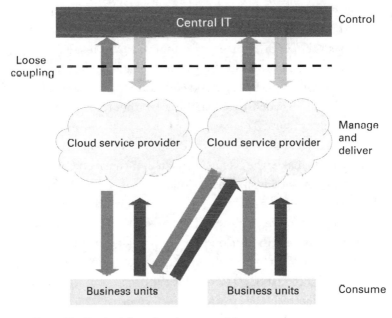

Figure 36 Service delivery based usage model

The usage model of figure 36 is distinct from the usage models previously discussed because its purpose is to especially address cloud services natively. The previous models were predicated on the use of traditional IT services or private cloud services. With the service delivery based usage model of figure 36, the central IT department maintains a catalog of cloud services and cloud service providers from which the business units can choose; the business units engage directly with the cloud service providers in terms of the billing and SLAs. The central IT department then subsumes the role of the service integrator. As the adoption of this model evolves in the workplace, and traditional IT is eventually replaced by cloud computing, the role of central IT should evolve to a distributed, rather than a central, function as figure 37 shows.

Having a distributed IT function embedded in the business units makes the business much more agile and able to fully exploit the advantages of cloud computing. The IT function would then be led by a chief technologist who would be responsible for defining the standards within the organization to engage with the cloud service providers. Secondarily, his role would be to provide governance and auditing in order to ensure that the services and the business units follow the defined technology standards. The other, traditional, functions of the central IT department such as billing and IT contract management simply become incorporated with the finance and procurement departments, respectively. It

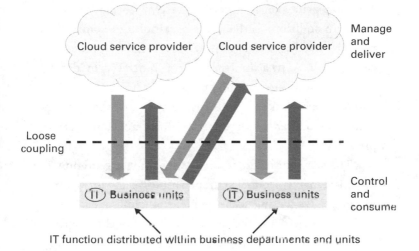

Figure 37 Service consumption based usage model

is this minimalist vision of IT that cloud computing enables. And that is one of the main reasons why cloud computing presents such a paradigm shift for the workplace and businesses in general: it devolves the control of IT from a select few residing in a central IT department to the many users of IT within the business departments!

Interoperability

As you will have gathered from the previous discussion, each of the usage models we considered had an underlying common principle: for every service to coexist with another. In addition, for business continuity or commercial reasons, you might also want to ensure that a cloud service can be replaced by a similar one from another provider. All this calls for interoperability between services.

Interoperability is the capability to use the same or similar cloud services offered by different cloud service providers.

The scope of interoperability does not extend only to technical matters, but also to such topics as the integration of billing, reporting, management, business processes, and, of course, data. And this is regardless of the cloud delivery model used—private, public, hybrid, or community. The following section heads constitute a checklist that you can adopt and extend to ensure that your cloud services have interoperability.

Governance and Auditing

If you are using an auditing process and policy for one cloud service, then you should ensure that any other services you procure to interoperate with your current cloud service also conform to that same auditing standard. Similarly, for governance, you need to ensure that the same governance board within your organization has oversight of all the cloud services, especially those that need to meet interoperability requirements.

Compliance

If you need to comply with industry or countrywide regulations, then you should establish whether the cloud services you use come under their scope. If they do, then all the cloud services that need to interoperate have to comply with the same regulations. Generally, from a cloud services perspective, there tends to be a gradation between general regulations and industry-specific regulations as the cloud service becomes more specialist in nature. This is shown in figure 38 where general, utility, services like email and office productivity have global scope and a requirement to abide by general, international, laws and regulations. When more specialist cloud services are considered, local

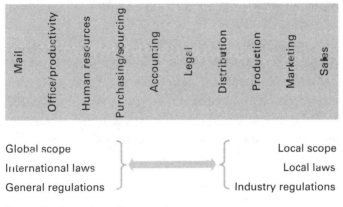

Figure 38 General compliance requirements

laws and industry regulations normally apply. This is a general observation that may not always apply to a specific cloud service, however.

Security and Data Integrity

For data integrity, the same encryption standards and schemes need to be in place across the cloud services that need to interoperate. Otherwise, data flow will not occur seamlessly. For security, you will need to ensure that the same security procedures are in place in order for there not to be a disparity in the security levels between the interoperable cloud services. You should also ensure that the users of all the services have common security training because it is best to standardize on a single security policy within an organization.

Data Integration

For seamless data integration between cloud services, two factors are important: a common format and a common data model. Format refers to the way data are presented; a spreadsheet stores information in a different format to a text file, for instance. Even when you have the same format, there needs to be commonality about what the data relates to. For example, if you have two text files (notice that both have the same format) but one file contains information about your inventory whereas the other one contains information about your salary, then both have dissimilar data models. So you need to ensure that the cloud services that interoperate use the same data format and models.

Process Integration

Besides having the same data format and model for interoperability, you need to ensure that tasks are carried out by the cloud services for the same business process. This is process integration. There are two aspects to process integration. One is where you want one process in a cloud service to receive data from another and commence a workflow that is an extension of the first process; the other aspect is when you want both processes to be the same so that you may interchange them, almost in a plug-and-play manner. For both aspects, you will need to ensure that the processes use the same business process language (BPL) and protocol in order for your cloud services to be interoperable. To make things easy with data and process integration, an enterprise service bus (ESB) is usually used to ensure that many of the technical integration concerns are hidden at a lower layer of abstraction.

Business Continuity

There are two aspects to business continuity. One is related to disaster recovery where you would want to use a secondary cloud service, most likely from a different service provider, in order to ensure that minimal disruption to your cloud service. Another aspect concerns the need to use a secondary cloud service provider in case the current one cannot meet a spike in your capacity demand. Both aspects can use cloud bursting to ensure seamless flow of control from one cloud to another. However, the capability to use cloud bursting or some such automated method of using a similar cloud service between different vendors needs to be in place. This is much more a technical requirement that uses the right protocol and standards to ensure that control passes from one cloud service to another seamlessly. In addition, it is likely that data and process integration requirements shall have to be met in order to permit business continuity.

Monitoring and Alerting

In the future, cloud services are expected to become self-healing in that the monitoring and remediation processes will become automated. But until that happens, you need to ensure that any alerts arising from the monitoring of your cloud services use a common standard and format for communication to your team. This way your team will be able to respond to the alerts in a timely manner. You can also be proactive here by performing certain tests on a regular basis. These tests could be, for example, stress tests to ensure that you have the right capacity for serving your customers or penetration tests to assess whether any security gaps exist that might result in a security breach.

In the future, cloud services are expected to become self-healing in that the monitoring and remediation processes will become automated.

Billing and Reporting

The billing processes, formats, and reports (I am using this generically to denote statements and invoices) should all be similar between the services in order for you to assess their total cost of ownership in a meaningful and rapid way. You may also need to ensure that the people that work with billing have a common understanding of the processes and reports in order for you to have interoperability not only with the processes and reports but also with people.

Business Processes

Transitioning to the cloud gives you a good opportunity to re-design your business processes in order to make them more efficient. Processes connect different parts of a business and so improving them should improve your whole business. And cloud computing can be an excellent enabler in re-engineering a business because of the automated business processes that you can have using a BPaaS cloud. Even if you do not go all the way to BPaaS, you can still derive greater efficiencies in your processes through the onboarding of INaaS and SaaS cloud services—and thereby effect business change.

The business process re-design (BPR) model (created by Hammer and Champy) shown in figure 39 provides a good procedure for re-designing your business processes.[3] The main idea in adopting the BPR model is that attempts

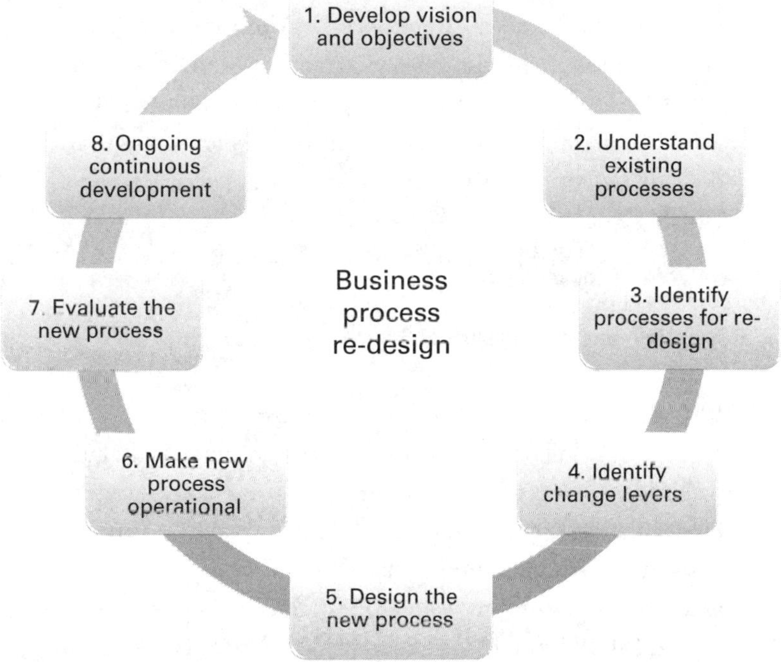

Figure 39 Business process re-design model

to improve the efficiency of organizations can only succeed if the processes are also improved. (This also applies to IoT related processes as the machine to machine interactions need to be similarly efficient.) Thus, when using the BPR model, one of the questions asked (during step 3 of figure 39) is whether a process, or one of its workflows, is necessary. Only those deemed necessary are kept, improved, and implemented. At step 5, you will design some of the processes as BPaaS cloud services in their entirety, some as using one of the cloud service models, and others outside the cloud. The criteria that you use to assess whether a service ought to have a cloud computing component are defined by your requirements and critical success factors, which we outline next.

Requirements and Critical Success Factors

When transitioning to the cloud or considering a new cloud service, you will need to have a set of requirements that will provide you with a yardstick for comparing cloud services. Additionally, the requirements will help you to crystallize your SLAs so that you may assess whether a cloud service is appropriate for you. Remember, cloud computing does not fulfill all your IT or computational needs; there will be instances, such as where very high-speed computing or resilience is needed, when you will want to use traditional computing. Given below is a checklist that can help you define your requirements for cloud computing. You can also use the requirements to define the critical success factors for the cloud services that you purchase. I have classified them into three categories: functional, non-functional, and business-related requirements. They are generic enough for you to use them for all the deployment and service models of cloud computing.

1. Functional requirements

   - Maturity

   - Interoperability

   - Feature-set

   - Usage model

2. Non-functional requirements

   - Security

   - Availability

   - Resilience

   - Network capacity

3. Business requirements

   - Price and value models

   - Risks

   - Business continuity

   - Support model

   - Reporting and billing

You can create a score matrix by scoring each of the requirements from, say, 0 to 3, with 0 denoting that a requirement is not met and 3 denoting a requirement being met entirely. Also each requirement could be weighted to reflect what you consider to be most important. For instance, maturity might have a weighting of 0 if that requirement is not at all important to you, but resilience might have a weighting of 3 to denote its high importance. Multiplying the weighting with the score will then provide you with a weighted rating for that particular requirement when comparing cloud services or their vendors.

Cloud Maturity Model

Figure 40 shows a maturity model for cloud computing. It has five levels of maturity: performed, defined, managed, adapted, and optimized (the highest level of maturity). The primary two rows of the table, titled "focus" and "success factors," describe the level of maturity in terms of its main characteristics and benefits, respectively. The last five rows consider the maturity characteristics of your cloud service in terms of (1) the people engaged to purchase, use, and manage the cloud services; (2) the processes that interact with the cloud services; (3) the financial and usage monitoring and reporting of the services; (4) the security, regulatory, functional and financial oversight that is provided

Maturity level	1. Performed	2. Defined	3. Managed	4. Adapted	5. Optimized
Focus	Functional; meets business needs on an ad hoc basis	Competent in saving costs and securing assets	Effective alignment to business needs	Responsive to business needs	Automated business functions
Success factors	New (or consolidated) business processes	Cost effective due to standardization	Agile, flexible, and reduced time-to-market	Measurable and repeatable outcomes	Continuous improvement built in
People	• No team in place • Little or no knowledge of cloud computing	• Basic roles and responsibilities defined	• Regular training in place • Roles and responsibilities being practiced	• Knowledge management in place • Incentives for cloud service reuse in place	• New optimized cloud services implemented
Processes	• No interoperability standards defined • Cloud service reuse and life cycle not defined	• Data and process interoperability defined • Best practices defined • Service life cycle defined	• Cloud service reuse being evangelized • Data and process interoperability in place	• BPR model followed • Business activity monitored for key processes	• Agile and optimized processes in place • Business processes continuously improved
Monitoring and reporting	• No or minimal monitoring • Reporting mostly relegated to billing	• Metrics and KPIs defined	• Metrics and KPIs reported	• Metrics and KPIs tracked	• Metrics continuously optimized to meet business needs
Governance	• No clear ownership of the cloud service	• Ownership is defined • Sponsorship from top management	• Governance process defined and followed • Communication plan in place	• Metrics and KPIs governed across all business units	• Federated governance with all business units in place
Financial control	• Usually based on credit cards	• Billing and related utilization statements tracked	• Penalties and chargebacks defined	• Financial planning and budgeting in place for use of cloud services	• Cloud computing considered a profit center as it becomes part of the business model

Figure 40 Cloud maturity model

to ensure that the cloud services meet your needs; and (5) the financial management in place to ensure that the cloud services remain financially viable. The maturity levels are not mutually exclusive for these five characteristics; you can have a maturity level of 1 for people and a maturity level of 3 for processes, for example. However, the overall maturity of your cloud service would be denoted as that level at which most characteristics coincide.

You can use the maturity model in two ways: first, to create a strategy to improve your use and commissioning of cloud services—this will enable you to transition from one maturity level to a higher one; second, to understand best-practice cloud computing. Obviously, the final column, describing the optimized maturity level, should be considered as the ultimate goal.

FUTURE OUTLOOK

Cloud computing is an enabling technology for automation and abstraction. This places it in a unique position to effect paradigm shifts related to your work, society, and life. This chapter discusses some emerging technologies and trends that are related to cloud computing; they are the catalysts of change for the future technology landscape. I discuss these trends and make some extrapolations to what could happen in future. Of course, as with predictions in general, not all may come to pass. Nevertheless, it is always good to know the art of the possible and what doors cloud computing may open for us in shaping the future.

Internet of Things and Services

In your home, you will find many appliances that contain microprocessors and microcontrollers: ovens, washing machines, televisions, refrigerators, and even some rubbish bins. And this list is set to increase due to the very low prices of microcontrollers. It would not be surprising if disposable items such as lightbulbs started to include such devices. When you connect these appliances to the Internet, you get connected devices, and the network they use is called the "Internet of Things," or IoT. Why should you want to connect such devices to the Internet? Let us consider your rubbish bin as an example. What if it became full and its sensor could let the facilities department in your locality know that this is the case, then they could empty the bins when needed rather than send out a van on a regular basis. Further suppose that your bin could predict when it would become full (it can do this simply by extrapolating the average increase in weight that it sensed on a daily basis) and then send out an email or a signal to let the facilities department know a few days in advance. This way the department could plan ahead and ensure that an optimum refuse collection route is in place. This would save fuel and time for your locality. As a result your local taxes may be reduced (or perhaps not increase) so that you may benefit too. Something similar is already happening with your printers at your workplace. The printers monitor the paper, ink, and toner—known as consumable resources—and send out an email to a central desk when these are about to run out. The printer's replacement ink and toner are then sent out to your facilities department for replacement. And your company does not get charged for these services! This is because the printer is "owned" by the printer company and leased out to your work company. Your company simply pays the printer company a monthly amount that is based on the number of pages printed in that month. Thus the IoT printer has a cloud-based utility price model. The monitoring of a large number of printers, sending out bills on the basis of pages printed per month and also the automated ordering of supplies such as ink can be thought of as a business process, or a service. When such a service is automated in the cloud and is there purely to support IoT devices, then you have an "Internet of Services," or IoS. Another example of an IoS is when you have a large number of streetlights in a particular locality connected to the Internet. They are monitored for the replacement of lightbulbs in an automated manner, thus obviating the need for a person to go out regularly on an inspection tour. Additionally the streetlights could have multiple uses: collection of weather-related information on temperature, condensation, and atmospheric pressure, or even counting the number of passers-by in order to assess the convenience of certain roads. In any case, the monitoring of the streetlights for lightbulb replacement would be an IoS for the various IoT connected lamps. As you can tell from these examples, IoT and IoS are related and so should be considered together.

Cloud of Things and Services (CoTS)

What have IoT and IoS got to do with cloud computing, you may well ask. Well, the processing that takes place by monitoring the IoT devices and executing the services, as part of a workflow, to support those IoT devices will usually be in the cloud. This is where the IoS type services will reside. So the IoT devices and their related IoS type services will have their own cloud. Such a cloud can be a private, public, community, or hybrid cloud depending on the application and your need. I have coined the term "Cloud of things and services," or CoTS, to refer to such a specialist cloud. Even though there may be few, if any, CoTS at present, they will become ubiquitous in future with the proliferation of IoT devices and their IoS services. The key premise of CoTS is automation. This supports the dual premises of IoT and IoS: convenience and service when and where needed. The "where" is important in the premise. Considering our example of the streetlight, you will know the exact lamp (and its location) that requires a replacement lightbulb when needed. For nonstationary devices, geo-positioning using the GPS[1] may be used to obtain the exact geo-location of the IoT device in terms of longitude, latitude, and elevation. The ubiquitous characteristic of cloud computing has considerable synergy with IoT devices because of the need to monitor them and provide services related to them wherever they may be.

Some broad areas where CoTS based services can be provided are:

1. *Smart home*   Nest smoke detector and fire alarm system are examples of connected devices within the home or office.

2. *Wearables*   Google Glass and Apple iWatch are good examples of these. They provide a platform not only for communication but also for sensors to monitor your health or environment.

3. *Smart city*   Traffic management, water distribution, waste management, urban security, environmental moni toring, pedestrian congestion management, and street lighting are some example use cases of connecting a CoTS service to IoT devices.

4. *Smart grids*   Smart metering augmented with IoT services for information about electricity consumption to improve the efficiency, reliability, and economics of electricity usage.

5. *Retail*   Proximity-based advertising, smart wallets, and NFC[2] related purchasing in the retail sector.

The above list is just the tip of the iceberg; it can easily be extended to cover IoT services in areas such as Banking, Manufacturing, Healthcare, Farming and Transport.

Personal Clouds

If you can have a cloud for things, then why not have a cloud for people? A personal cloud is one that you own and use for your personal needs. Examples are plentiful: (1) storing documents (your statements, driving license, etc.); (2) storing your electronic wallet (e.g., your financial wallet or your health wallet); (3) storing your shopping basket for electronic shopping; and (4) storing your music and videos (e.g., Amazon's Cloud Drive and Apple's iCloud). Consider the use case of your health wallet. With the onset of IoT and Wearable devices, it is becoming common for people to measure various health metrics such as blood pressure, heart rate, and weight so that they may be stored in a health wallet. Microsoft, Google, and Apple are developing, if not trialing, such wallets. If you automate the monitoring of your health metrics using IoT and wearables, then you have an interesting intersection between the personal cloud and CoTS. Your health wallet is a personal cloud, but because it connects with IoT devices and obtains your health data, it is a CoTs as well. The CoTs would have a service (remember IoS) that would alert you, your doctor, or your family if the health metrics traverse a certain level. But you can take this service one step further by using predictive analytics. What if you received an alert that told you of an impending deterioration in your health as a factor of a combination of metrics? You could then be proactive and ensure that your health improved by addressing the factors that produced the alert.

Efficiencies of Experience

In the mid-1960s, Boston Consulting Group (BCG) developed an idea that they called the experience curve: the more experience an organization gains in producing a particular product or service, its costs become lower in delivering that service. As time progresses and cloud service providers gain experience, the cloud services' costs ought to decline. The BCG found that costs characteristically decline by 20 to 30 percent in real terms each time accumulated experience doubles. This means that once inflation is factored out, costs should always decline. However, the rate of decline depends on growth; if growth is fast, then costs decline fast as well. In any case, this idea was found to apply across a broad range of industries, products, and services. There is a caveat, though. Different services and products have different slopes for the experience curve, and so different factors for cost reduction.[3]

Figure 41 shows the effect of the experience curve in terms of the "costs" expressed as the need for a greater skillset and the effort required to be expended in using a cloud service. At point 1 in figure 41, there is a shift downward as more experience is gained over time and innovation is applied. This results in a lower technical skillset required in the use of cloud computing for the same effort or time.

Similarly point 3 shows the effect of the shift in the curve given the same technical skillset: less time or effort is needs to be expended in using the cloud service. Over time, this should translate into greater cost efficiencies for organizations that make use of cloud services.

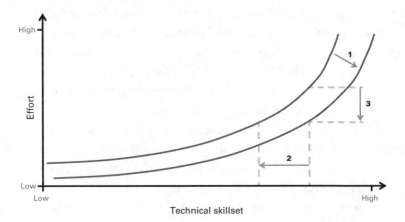

Figure 41   Experience curve embedded in cloud computing

A Cloud Service Exchange

I discuss an innovative idea that I have developed for purchasing cloud services using a cloud service exchange. Just as stocks are exchanged for money in a stock market, a cloud service exchange prices and exchanges services in real time, so cloud services can be bought and sold as commodities. This is easier for services that are at a lower abstraction layer, such as IaaS and PaaS, compared to higher level ones such as BPaaS. A major component of such an exchange would be the interoperability of the cloud services. Thus one service could be replaced by another seamlessly and instantaneously via the exchange. Service producers and consumers would then share the exchange platform in order to effect a deal, and each service would be classified in terms of the cloud patterns developed in chapter 2. The outcome would be a fair price for the cloud service user since the price paid would depend on the supply and demand parameters of a service. A real-time mechanism for price and service discovery would need to be implemented so that an instantaneous trade can be realized by matching the right service to its prospective buyer. This is something that the future could bring to the world of IT because cloud computing is the natural evolutionary step in the increasing commoditization of IT technologies and services.

AFTERWORD:
WHAT THE AUTHOR THINKS

This chapter discusses some economic, moral, and social issues that technology, IT, and especially cloud computing bring up. Many of these issues are intractable, and my objective is to inform you of the role that technology is playing in shaping our society and world. I outline below the influence and use of technology in discrete sections, mostly unrelated, from a social perspective.

Tool for Democracy

According to Bernays,[1] for the survival and operation of representative democracy, consent is engineered through the use of various propaganda techniques. These techniques, Bernays posits, become effective through the discovery of the hidden motives of the masses; enthusiastic and potent results are achieved if, by the judicious use of emotional arguments (artifices, perhaps), the available choices are limited to just two. (There is a reason why successful democracies have two large parties, incidentally.) In discovering those hidden motives—emotional buttons—of the masses, analysis of data plays a big role. Such analysis techniques on extremely large and multi-faceted aspects of data are known generically as big data. But the gathering of that data from various sources becomes a rather trivial task if there are just a few, but large, public clouds to mine. And so, once cloud computing grows and subsequently consolidates into a few major players, the gathering, processing, analyzing, and reporting of big data will become so much easier for various parties, political or otherwise, to manipulate opinion and further effect a dumbing down of the people.

The Big Divide

When the Great Recession started in 2007, the top 1 percent wealthiest people in United States held 34.6 percent of all its financial assets. Just four years later, in 2011, the top 1 percent of the population owned 42.7 percent of the wealth. Hence, wealth transferred from the rest of the population to the top 1 percent rather swiftly. This financial disparity between the wealthy and the poor has caused a lot of debate in various circles. Technology, interestingly, has increasingly been used during this time as a means to placate the populace. The idea being that even though the rich–poor gap might have increased over time and our standard of living (a metric based largely on income) might have been stagnant, our quality of life has increased because we live longer (thanks to advances in medicine), we have smartphones, we have electricity, cars, television, and so on. Generally, things that we did not have just a few decades ago that we currently take for granted—thanks to major advances in technology and medicine. Thus innovation and advances in technology have somehow been used as an excuse for not addressing the key factors that have led to the widening of the financial gap between the very rich and the rest of the people. In practice, there will always be a gap, and one may argue reasonably that having such a gap is needed in order to motivate the people to achieve higher goals in life. However, social commentators ought not to use technology and innovation as a crutch to put forward their arguments because that simply obfuscates[2] the debate and does not answer the main questions: (1) what is the cause of the widening gap, and (2) what extent of the gap makes a society unhealthy? Social and economic innovation ought to be pursued in order to address such issues instead of using advances in technology as excuses. Technology does not always have the answers even though it may be used as a tool to provide a solution to these types of questions.

However, the more technology advances—and cloud computing is such an advancement—the easier it becomes to placate the populace with a "feel-good" factor, in addition to the current opiates of sports and sex for the people.[3] These being tools used to maintain a docile population and enfranchise it in a process that is most likely skewed to widening the financial gap even further.

Another premise is that technology itself creates the divide because greater automation will mean that more mundane jobs will be replaced by machines. This means that those lacking the technical skills or the specialist talent that harnesses the use of technology will be either unemployed or underemployed. In contrast, those with advanced skills will be in great demand and the outcome will be a widening of the remuneration gap between these two groups, as discussed by Brynjolfsson and McAfee in their book *The Second Machine Age*.

Personal Information

Most major countries have easy access to your information. Your emails, your shopping habits, your bank information and financial details, your location, travel plans if booking a flight, as well as your activity. Much of this information is simply collected and probably not used in a deleterious manner. However, the question remains: Should a government, however benign, have the right to its citizens' data?

Despite most egalitarian countries having privacy laws, you will still find that the governments of those countries have easy access to all kinds of information about you. Generally, if something can be done easily and at almost no cost, then it usually will be done. As such, with the commoditizing of IT systems through the adoption of cloud computing, it is prudent to surmise that most governments, even those of minor countries, will have complete access to and knowledge of their citizens' personal lives in the near future. Recent events, such as those related to Edward Snowden, bear this out. There is an underlying assumption—whether right or wrong—that most governments espouse: the government has the right to listen to and gather data on its citizens, and there is something wrong with a citizen should they oppose this premise. In practice, there are always devious episodes (national security, terrorism, communism, etc.) in a country to marshal such thoughts among the cowed masses. Big Brother[4] therefore is a reality today and technology—especially cloud computing—plays a key role in making it so. And this is certain to increase in future as a result of the increasing sophistication of data analysis techniques for which cloud computing is an enabler.

Productivity

The personal computer has changed business and work practices in a very short period of time. At my first job in the mid-1980s, I would write reports and various documents on paper, which I would hand over to a typing pool. After some time, sometimes extending to a few days, I would receive my typed up report to check. If, upon reading it, I felt that there were some typographical errors or changes to be made, I would then re-submit a corrected report to the typing pool. Finally, when I was happy with the report, I would sign it and have it distributed. The report would be photo-copied for distribution purposes. The whole process was rather lengthy and cumbersome. Today there are no typing pools! And the distribution process is instantaneous due to emails. All this thanks to the personal computer.

In the 1990s, with the increased use of personal computers in business and work, a kind of revolution occurred in the workplace that essentially replaced a lot of the business processes. Presentations, reports, analyses using spreadsheets—all these have changed entirely the business landscape. In their wake, increased productivity followed. As a result we had a stock market bull run that began in the mid-1990s and culminated in the Internet boom of 2000. Cloud computing not only quickens the pace for business, as the personal computer did, but also is an enabler for greater automation. Any business that wishes to automate a process, introduce a new software application or use a business service does not have to invest in computing infrastructure. Instead, with the use of a monthly payment agreement, they can have massively scalable computing infrastructure available to them instantaneously. In the wake of this enabling technology, many business functions can and should be automated. The outcome will be increased productivity in the workplace, and you can expect another stock market bull run as a result. There might be social repercussions, perhaps, due to the displacement of work in the interim. However, newer types of jobs should be created that replace the old, process related, ones as long as the economic theory of elasticity of substitution[5] holds true.

Business Scalability

Technology has made this Earth a much smaller place. In the past, a new business might have taken a few years to reach a certain size, but it will now reach that size in just a few months, if that. This is not only related to technology. The reach and scale afforded by technology has been exploited by artists, authors, retailers, manufacturers, and a plethora of businesses and people. Take, for example, the author of the Harry Potter novels, J. K. Rowling. Her market is global, and she has made more money than any other author in the past, including Shakespeare, largely due to a broader market. Another example is the music industry. With music being available anywhere in the world from

Netflix, Amazon Prime, Apple iTunes, or Google Play, a music artist has global reach within a few milliseconds. With cloud computing, automated business processes and information availability will have just as much global reach. That is why cloud computing is the best route for an entrepreneur to kick start a new business rapidly and with minimum financial expenditure.

APPENDIX: BACKUP SCHEMES

We consider some of the nuances of backups in this appendix by first defining a fileset and then considering the three common types of backup schemes: full, differential, and incremental.

Filesets

Usually, in storage file systems, a file hierarchy exists. This hierarchy comprises of a series of directories that form a tree-like structure. Each directory will then contain other directories, files, or other file-system objects such as links to files or directories. A fileset provides a means of partitioning the file system at a finer granularity than the entire file system so that you may select files for backup purposes and set read/write permissions individually. Hence your backup fileset is a set of files and directories that you have selected to back up.

Full Backups

A full backup will back up your entire fileset every time you perform the backup. The advantages of a full backup are that all the files and directories are backed up to one backup set, which makes it easy for you to locate a particular file, and that files and directories are easily restored from a single backup set should you need to restore them. Its disadvantages are that it is more time-consuming than other backup schemes, and that full backups require more space when compared to the other backup schemes.

Differential Backups

A differential backup backs up files that have changed since the last full backup was performed. A full backup and its differential backup should therefore include all the files (changed and unchanged) in your file set. The advantages of differential backups are that they require less space than incremental backups, and that backup times are generally faster when compared to full and incremental backups. Their disadvantages are that restoring all your files may take considerably longer than a full backup, since you may need to restore both the last differential and full backup, and that restoring individual files or directories may take longer, since you have to locate them on either the differential or full backup sets.

Incremental Backups

An incremental backup provides a backup of files that have changed or are new since the last incremental backup. The first incremental backup performs a full back up as it backs up all the files in the file set; subsequent incremental backups thereafter back up only those files that have changed since the previous backup. Its advantages are: (a) backup time is faster compared to full backups, (b) it requires less space when compared to other backup schemes, and (c) you can keep several versions of the same files on different backup sets. Its disadvantages are that in order to restore all the files, you must have all of the incremental backups available, and that it may take longer to restore a specific file or directory, since you must search more than one backup set to find the latest version.

The Difference between Backups and Archives

Backups are meant for the rapid recovery of day-to-day data, or operational data, that are in current use. Archives are meant to store data that are not used regularly but that you wish to keep for regulatory or compliance reasons. For backups, speed of recovery is important as you would like to be up and running should disaster strike, whereas for archiving, the capability to perform fast searches in order to locate information that is required is far more important. As you will surmise from these differences, backups are performed regularly on data that change often. However, archival data does not change often, and your archive schedules need to be less frequent than backup ones. Hence your backup sets will have longevity measured in weeks or months while your archive sets will have retention periods measured in years and decades.

Backup Rotation

Backup rotation schemes originated when backup media were expensive and wore out due to re-use when using tapes to perform backups. These days it is far cheaper and easier to configure a disk array to store backups and to monitor the disks for failure. In fact this is the method that works well for cloud storage and backup service providers. However, you can utilize the concept governing rotation schemes by substituting tapes with cloud service providers so that you can have a backup scheme that does not rely on a single cloud backup provider.

The main purpose of a backup rotation scheme was to minimize the amount of storage media used for backup data. Such a scheme defines how and when a backup job is run and the period over which the data is retained. *For our purposes, however, the idea is to minimize the risk of dependency on a single location or cloud backup provider rather than to minimize backup media use.* The most common rotation schemes are FIFO (First-In, First-Out), Grandfather-Father-Son, and the Tower of Hanoi. Let us consider the first two below in the context of cloud-based backup service providers.

The FIFO rotation scheme, when performed on a weekly rotation, for example, would mean that you make a full backup every day using seven tapes using one fresh tape on each day. Then, on the eighth day, you would reuse the tape you used on the first day, and on the ninth day, you would reuse the second day's tape, and so on. In a cloud context, let us assume that you appoint two different cloud backup providers, denoted as Provider #1 and Provider #2. If you wanted to follow a full backup scheme, then you would backup to each provider on alternate days. So on the first day, you would use Provider #1 for a full backup, and on the second day, you would use Provider #2 for a full backup. However, for a differential backup, you would perform a full backup with Provider #1 on the first day of a week, and then every day until the end of the week, perform a differential backup. Then, on the second week, use Provider #2 in a similar fashion thus alternating between Provider #1 and Provider #2 on a weekly basis.

The Grandfather-Father-Son rotation scheme is based on a monthly-weekly-daily rotation scheme. Thus you could appoint three backup cloud providers such that the "grandfather" backup cloud kept your monthly backups, the "father" kept your weekly ones, and the "son" kept your daily backup sets.

NOTES

Chapter 1

1. Peter Mell and Timothy Grance, "The NIST Definition of Cloud Computing" (draft), http://www.nist.gov/customcf/get_pdf.cfm?pub_id=909616, accessed November 12, 2015.

2. Michael Armbrust, Armando Fox, Rean Griffith, Anthony D. Joseph, Randy H. Katz, Andrew Konwinski, Gunho Lee, David A. Patterson, Ariel Rabkin, Ion Stoica, and Matei Zaharia, "Above the Clouds: A Berkeley View of Cloud Computing," University of California at Berkeley, February 10, 2009.

Chapter 2

1. General Packet Radio Services (GPRS) is a wireless communication service that provides continuous connection to the Internet.

2. Gossen's First Law of Economics, referred to as the law of diminishing marginal utility, states that as you use more of something, each additional unit of it is worth less to you than the one before.

3. The Gang of Four (GoF) refers to the four authors (Gamma, Helm, Johnson, and Vlissides) of the book titled *Design Patterns*, which was published in 1995. The book was a seminal work that has since become the authoritative guide on software patterns.

Chapter 3

1. The hype curve is a graphical presentation developed by Gartner for representing adoption and maturity of emerging technologies through five phases of its life cycle: (1) technology trigger, (2) peak of inflated expectations, (3) trough of disillusionment, (4) slope of enlightenment, and (5) plateau of productivity.

2. Formally, a use case identifies, clarifies, and organizes a service's or system's requirements in a methodical manner. The use case is made up of a set of possible sequences of interactions between you and the service in a particular environment and related to a particular goal. Even the informal use you put a cloud service to or the requirement you have for it is considered to be a use case.

Chapter 4

1. Developed by Bruce Henderson of the Boston Consulting Group in the mid-1960s, the experience curve was shown to be applicable to a broad range of industries.

Chapter 5

1. Voice biometrics can be used for identification as well as verification. Identification determines an unknown speaker's identity. Authentication verifies whether a speaker's identity is correct. In either case, voice biometrics uses the acoustic properties of a person's voice to identify or authenticate since those properties are unique to every individual.

2. Cookies are stored in a text file used by the Internet browser but accessed by websites to provide persistence between your visits to the sites. A tracking cookie tracks the usage of your browser by recording your entries and sending the information to the cookie designer. Not all tracking cookies are malicious, although they can be used in such a manner.

3. Erika McCallister, Tim Grance, and Karen Scarfone, "Guide to Protecting the Confidentiality of Personally Identifiable Information (PII)," NIST Special Publication 800–122, April 2010.

4. Firmware refers to the software that resides within a device that provides its electronics with instructions to function as intended. Firmware is changed rarely, if at all, during a device's lifetime; some firmware is even permanently installed nonerasable memory (referred to as nonvolatile memory) and cannot be changed after manufacture.

5. VOIP stands for Voice-Over-Internet-Protocol; it sends voice traffic over the Internet so that you may have a conversation using software, for example, FaceTime or Skype.

Chapter 6

1. A thin-client device is one that has just the operating system and connectivity software installed on it and it is used to access applications that are hosted in the cloud. A Chromebook is an example of a thin-client device.

2. A zero-client device is one that just has the bare minimum CPU with the connectivity embedded in hardware; the operating system as well as the applications reside in the cloud.

3. Also known as a fat client, a thick-client application performs most or all of its functions independently without the assistance of external resources. A

thin-client application, in contrast, performs little processing on its own and depends on a server to perform the computing functions; it simply acts as a conduit to the server by providing input data that need to be processed.

4. An integrated development environment (IDE) is an application that provides facilities for software development. IDE normally consists of a source code editor (usually this incorporates intelligent code completion), build automation tools, a compiler, or interpreter, and a debugger. Additionally, it offers facilities such as visual programming, code analysis, and unit testing.

5. Services that perform a single task as part of an application are called *micro-services*. In cloud computing, a cloud cell should be used to provide such micro-services.

Chapter 7

1. Also known as an acquiring bank, an acquirer processes payments to merchants for products or services.

Chapter 10

1. A strategy is best defined as a workable sequence of actions that follow a plan designed to achieve a distinct, measurable goal.

2. Shadow IT, along with stealth IT, describes services used by business departments without the explicit knowledge or approval of the central IT department.

3. For details, refer to Michael Hammer and James Champy, *Reengineering the Corporation: A Manifesto for Business Revolution* (New York: HarperCollins, 2006).

Chapter 11

1. Global Positioning System (GPS) is an American satellite-based system that provides location and time information anywhere on or near the Earth as long as there is an unobstructed line of sight to four or more geo-positioning satellites. Similar systems have been developed by Russia (GLONASS) and China (BeiDou) using a constellation of satellites; Indian (IRNSS) and European (Galileo) systems are also under development.

2. Near field communications is a technology that detects and identifies you, when you are in its proximity, in order to initiate an instantaneous payment.

3. See the article by Pankaj Ghemawat, "Building Strategy on the Experience Curve," *Harvard Business Review* 63, no. 2 (March–April 1985).

Afterword

1. See *Propaganda*, by Edward Bernays (Routledge, 1928).

2. See Robert Thouless's book *Straight and Crooked Thinking* in which he considers this tangential argument as a dishonest trick of extension in an argument (chapter 7, 2011 edition; chapter 3, original 1930 edition).

3. The economist Karl Marx is famously quoted as saying that "Religion is the opium of the people." This might have been true in the nineteenth century but, in my opinion, no longer holds true today since sex and sports have become the new opiates during these increasingly hedonistic times.

4. In George Orwell's book, titled *Nineteen Eighty-Four*, Big Brother is a leader of a totalitarian state in which the citizens live under constant monitoring and surveillance—ostensibly for their own good.

5. The economic interpretation of "elasticity of substitution" is that capital and labor have a somewhat efficient commutability in the production process. Thus, freed capital as a result of increased productivity and the operating expenditure based price models of cloud computing should translate into more jobs.

GLOSSARY

Aggregation   A relationship that denotes "is-a." Thus a forest is an aggregate of trees. The underlying assumption here is that all the trees are similar in terms of their attributes or properties. Should the trees be of varying types, with different features that you need to use, then aggregation no longer applies. Instead, the relationship then is said to be composition.

BPaaS   Business process as a service; see **Service model**.

CapEx   Capital expenditure. The up-front expense borne by you or a third party to create a product or service. Also referred to as the "implementation costs" or the "non-recurring costs."

Change management   Change management concerns the addition, modification, or removal of services or service components while reducing incidents, disruption, and rework.

Cloud bursting   A cloud service or application that instantaneously jumps (bursts out) to use the resources of another cloud. It would do this in order to meet an inordinate increase in demand or due to business continuity reasons.

Cloud cell   A new concept developed in this book to denote a discrete cloud service that performs a single business or technical function. It can be an implementation of a micro-service in the cloud. A number of cloud cells could be used together to provide a conglomerate, unique, cloud service. Cloud cells can have relationships with other cells such as composition, encapsulation, and federation.

Cloud service   Implementation of a business process—through a set of related functional components and resources—that provides business value to the end consumer of the service. It can be categorized in terms of five service models.

Community cloud   A shared cloud computing service that is targeted to a limited group whose members share the same need or use case. These can be diverse and can vary from business needs (compliance requirements) to individual (a hobby or a pension fund) to societal needs (a state or nation).

Composition   A relationship that denotes "has-a." Thus a car is a composition of a number of distinct units, such as steering wheel, tires, bonnet, doors. Each unit that creates the composed object has its own distinct attributes or properties.

Currency   Refers to how technically current computational resources are. Currency is usually considered in terms of version numbers of the software and the generation of the hardware.

Delivery model   Efficient combination of end-to-end processes, methodologies, and quality procedures, together with the right skills on a global basis, that enable your IT department to meet its business needs.

Elasticity   The use of horizontal scalability to scale out your cloud service when demand is high and scale in when demand is low.

Encapsulation   Denotes either the composition or the aggregation of cloud services. The concept is derived from object-oriented programming and design where an object can encapsulate another.

Federation   This is a when you create a composite cloud service by an alliance with other, disparate, clouds or cloud cells. Although these would usually be provided by different cloud service providers, they can well be a mixture of your own cloud cells as well as a third party's cloud cells.

Hybrid cloud   Combination of private and public cloud services based on a policy-driven, coordinated approach to the consumption and management of those cloud services.

IaaS   Infrastrusture as a service; see **Service model**.

INaaS   Information as a service; see **Service model**.

Interoperability   Capability to use the same or similar cloud services offered by different cloud service providers. Relies on billing, management, reporting, data, and application or process functions to be in place.

ITIL   Information Technology Infrastructure Library. It is a framework that provides guidance on the full life cycle of defining, developing, managing, delivering, and improving IT services from an operational perspective rather than a delivery perspective. ITIL is descriptive rather than prescriptive as it provides best-practice advice on IT service management.

Maturity model   A model that gauges your maturity in the use and management of cloud computing services and points out the areas of improvement. It allows your organization to have its methods and processes assessed according to best practice against a clear set of benchmarks.

Multi-tenancy   Pooling of resources, virtual or physical, such as software, storage, or virtual machines, to provide a shared common service to each user of the cloud service.

OLA   Operational level agreement. This is an internal agreement between the supplier and internal consumer (or re-supplier to the end consumer) within an organization that needs to provide a service to the end consumer.

OpEx   Operating expenditure. The ongoing, operational, costs that you incur when consuming a cloud service. Also referred to as "runtime costs" or the "recurring costs."

PaaS   Platform as a service; see **Service model**.

Private cloud   A form of cloud computing that is used by only one entity. The entity can be an organization, person, or thing. The private cloud ensures that the cloud computing resources are shared only by cloud services meant for that entity, as demand dictates.

Public cloud   A form of cloud computing that is shared by a number of entities. An entity can be an organization, person, or thing. The public cloud ensures that the cloud computing resources are pooled together for the use of the entities as demand dictates.

Roadmap   Future plan for upgrading and updating the cloud components.

SaaS   Software as a service; see **Service model**.

Service   A collection of IT systems, components, and resources that work together in order to provide value to the end user or consumer. Also see **Cloud service**.

Service model   There are five service models of cloud computing: IaaS, PaaS, SaaS, INaaS, and BPaaS. A service model is the type of cloud service that you can use or create.

SLA   Service level agreement. This is a contract, usually written, between the service consumer and the service supplier in terms of how quickly the service will be delivered (when), its quality (what), and scope (where and how much).

SLO   Service level objective. This is a metric used by a service provider to measure their performance to ensure that they meet the SLA or the OLA.

Thin client   May refer to a device, an application, or a service. A thin-client device does not have an application installed on it. You use the thin client device to access a remote application or service that may be hosted in the cloud. A thin client application or service is one that is hosted on a server (in traditional hosting) or the cloud and can be accessed either using a thin or fat client device.

Zero client   Similar to a thin client device except that its operating system and browser are embedded in the hardware.

BIBLIOGRAPHY

Cloud Computing Books

Most books on cloud computing delve deep into technologies that underpin cloud computing and its application from a technical standpoint. Some books do consider the business-related aspects of cloud computing, however, and these are listed here.

Bahga, Arshdeep, and Vijay Madisetti. *Cloud Computing: A Hands-On Approach.* CreateSpace, 2013.

Erl, Thomas. *Cloud Computing: Concepts, Technology and Architecture.* Englewood Cliffs, NJ: Prentice Hall, 2013.

Fehling, Cristoph. *Cloud Computing Patterns: Fundamentals to Design, Build, and Manage Cloud Applications.* Vienna: Springer, 2014.

Gautam, Shroff. *Enterprise Cloud Computing: Technology, Architecture, Applications.* Cambridge, UK: Cambridge University Press, 2010.

Hugos, Hulitzky. *Business in the Cloud.* Hoboken, NJ: Wiley, 2010.

Kavis, Michael. *Architecting the Cloud.* Hoboken, NJ: Wiley, 2014.

Mulholland, Andy, and Jon Pyke. *Enterprise Cloud Computing: A Strategy Guide for Business and Technology Leaders.* Tampa, FL: Meghan-Kiffer Press, 2010.

Rafaels, Ray. *Cloud Computing: From Beginning to End.* CreateSpace, 2015.

Rhoton, John. *Cloud Computing Explained*, 2nd ed. London: Recursive Press, 2009.

Sosinsky, Barrie. *Cloud Computing Bible.* Indianapolis, IN: Wiley, 2011.

Weinman, Joe. *Cloudonomics: The Business Value of Cloud Computing.* Hoboken, NJ: Wiley, 2012.

Other Books

These books are worth reading for a better understanding of the wider social impact and political aspects of technology. Brealy's book on corporate finance is worthwhile when considering the derivation of utility-based price models on the basis of the time value of money.

Bernays, Edward. *Propaganda*. New York: Horace Liveright, 1928.

Brealy, Richard, Stewart Myers, and Alan Marcus. *Fundamentals of Corporate Finance*, 7th ed. Boston: McGraw-Hill, 2011.

Brynjolfsson, Erik, and Andrew McAfee. *The Second Machine Age: Work, Progress, and Prosperity in a Time of Brilliant Technologies*. New York: Norton, 2014.

Hayek, F. A. *The Road to Serfdom*. London: Routledge Classics, 2003.

Orwell, George. *Nineteen Eighty-Four*. New York: Harcourt Brace, 1949.

Samuelson, Paul, and William Nordhaus. *Economics*, 19th ed. Boston: McGraw-Hill, 2009.

Thouless, Robert. *Straight and Crooked Thinking*. New York: Simon and Schuster, 1932.

Blogs and Websites

Various websites that give a broader perspective of the technologies, standards, and policies that drive cloud computing are listed below.

A Hacker's Perspective Blog. http://blog.dt.org.

Association of Computer Machinery. https://www.acm.org.

Forrester Research. https://www.forrester.com/home.

Free Software Foundation (FSF). https://www.fsf.org.

Gartner Technology Research. http://www.gartner.com/technology/home.jsp.

National Institute of Standards and Technology (NIST); Information Technology Lab. http://www.nist.gov/itl/cloud/index.cfm.

The Open Group Open Platform 3.0™ Forum. http://www.opengroup.org/subjectareas/platform3.0.

Technology News Websites

These websites are useful for monitoring the latest developments in the fast paced world of cloud computing and related technologies.

Ars Technica. http://arstechnica.com.

CNet. http://www.cnet.com.

InfoWorld. http://www.infoworld.com.

ReadWrite. http://readwrite.com.

TechCrunch. http://techcrunch.com.

The Register. http://www.theregister.co.uk.

Ziff-Davis Technology News Network. http://www.zdnet.com.

INDEX

NAYAN B. RUPARELIA is an entrepreneur and Chief Technology Officer in England. He has more than thirty years of experience in technology, and from 2007 to 2015 he was Chief Technologist at Hewlett Packard Enterprise.